HUMAN RESOURCE CETIFICATION INSTITUTE

CERTIFICATION GUIDE

Raymond B. Weinberg, CCP, SPHR

ISBN 1-58644-023-3

Printed in the United States of America
Seventh Edition, 2002

TABLE OF CONTENTS

PREFACE

To stay current in the human resource (HR) management field, individuals must continually update their knowledge and skills. The twenty-first century workplace will require HR professionals to respond to such widely varying concerns as the changing nature of work, reengineered workplaces, virtual offices, the boundary-less organization, employee rights, worker literacy, and global competition--to name just a few.

As the profession changes, so does the body of knowledge that HR professionals must master. Consequently, through extensive research conducted by the Human Resource Certification Institute (HRCI), efforts to identify the HR body of knowledge have been undertaken. From this process, new and revised test specifications are developed and updated in all HR functional areas. These specifications form the blueprint for development of the HRCI certification examinations.

HRCI exists to enhance the professionalism of HR practitioners, educators, researchers, and consultants through its certification process. A key part of that process is providing professional certification examinations. Depending on experience levels, individuals in the profession can attain certification as either a Professional in Human Resources (PHR) or a Senior Professional in Human Resources (SPHR). This guide is an aid to candidates considering taking one of the examinations. It is designed to help understand the certification process, allow candidates to assess their levels of preparedness; and to determine which areas may need additional review.

ACKNOWLEDGMENTS

This publication would not have been possible without the contribution of the HRCI Board of Directors and the many volunteers who help in item and test development. It is the work product of these volunteers that serves as the basis for the content of this Certification Guide.

Volunteers are the heart of HRCI's certification program. All are certified professionals who have successfully passed the HRCI certification examination. They write and review draft test items, establish passing or cut scores, and otherwise support the Institute in its mission.

SECTION I:

CERTIFICATION GUIDE

CERTIFICATION GUIDE

This guide was developed with a number of purposes in mind. First, it was designed to provide HR professionals with relevant information about HRCI and its certification process. Second, it describes the Institute's practice analysis process and its results – test specifications based on the human resource management body of knowledge. Third, it explains various ways to prepare for an HRCI certification examination. Finally, it provides a practice examination so individuals can assess their mastery of the HR body of knowledge.

HR practitioners historically site two primary reasons why they are reluctant to take one of the HRCI certification examinations. First, there is fear of the unknown, such as not knowing what to study or what types of questions will be asked. Another closely related fear is the fear of failure – not knowing one's level of proficiency before taking the examination. These two fears, whether real or imagined, prevent many capable HR practitioners from taking one of the certification examinations. This book was designed to alleviate these fears.

This publication is a starting point for formal training or informal self-development for persons interested in individual or group study in the human resource field.

Copies of the Certification Guide may be purchased from the SHRMStore, PO Box 930132, Atlanta, GA 31193-0132, 1-800-444-5006 or ordered online at www.shrm.org/shrmstore. Proceeds from the sales of this book are used to support the educational purposes and operations of the Institute. Inquiries about the certification program may be addressed to:

Human Resource Certification Institute
1800 Duke Street
Alexandria, VA 22314
(703) 548-3440
Fax #(703) 535-6474
TDD # (703) 548-6999
E-mail: info@hrci.org
HRCI homepage: http://www.hrci.org

SECTION II:

HUMAN RESOURCE PROFESSIONALISM

HUMAN RESOURCE PROFESSIONALISM

In the mid 1960's, the American Society for Personnel Administration (now the Society for Human Resource Management), in conjunction with Cornell University, approached the United States Department of Labor with a simple question – "What constitutes a profession?" The Department of Labor said there were five distinct characteristics that separate a profession from other pursuits or endeavors:

1. **National Organization** — A profession is defined by the existence of a national organization that can speak as a unified voice for its members and foster the development of the field. The Society for Human Resource Management (SHRM), with a membership exceeding 165,000, fulfills that role for the human resource management profession.

2. **Code of Ethics** — A profession has a code of ethics that identifies standards of behavior relating to fairness, justice, truthfulness, and social responsibility. SHRM has developed such a code to which all members are expected to adhere.

HRCI has also developed the following Model of Professional Excellence that includes ethical standards.

HRCI MODEL OF PROFESSIONAL EXCELLENCE

As certified human resource professionals, our personal standards of honor and integrity must, at all times, be above reproach and we must conduct ourselves in a manner that reflects favorably on our profession.

By adhering to the highest standard of honor and integrity, we as human resource professionals help to create an ethical climate within our organizations.

We have a duty to protect the interests of our employees, the organization and society to promote and encourage:

- Honesty and trustworthiness in all working relationships;
- Reliability in performing our assigned responsibilities;

- Truthfulness and accuracy in what is said and written;

- Constructiveness and cooperation in working relationships;

- Fairness, consideration, and non-discrimination in how we treat others;

- Adherence to the law in all activities;

- Economical use of resources;

- Commitment to excellence in the performance of our work; and

- Respect for the privacy of others.

3. **Research** — A profession is also marked by the existence of applied research related to the field. The SHRM Foundation funds research into new and emerging areas of HR. HRCI provides financial support to the SHRM Foundation in its pursuit of advancing the HR field. In addition, SHRM established a dedicated research department in 2000.

4. **Body of Knowledge** — A profession has a defined body of knowledge. HRCI, through its practice analysis study, defines the HR body of knowledge for practitioners in the field. This body of knowledge (the basis of the Institute's test specifications) is disseminated to professionals through publications, many of which are sponsored by SHRM.

5. **Credentialing** — Lastly, a profession has a credentialing organization that sets professional standards in the field. HRCI fulfills this requirement.

Together, SHRM, the SHRM Foundation and HRCI meet all of the requirements that define the human resource field as a profession. Although still a developing profession, the high standards set by these organizations, plus the high level of performance expected of a human resource professional, will make the challenge of professionalism that much greater in the future.

HUMAN RESOURCE CERTIFICATION INSTITUTE

HRCI, an affiliate of the Society for Human Resource Management (SHRM), is a non-profit organization whose purpose is to develop and maintain professional standards in the human resource (HR) field. This purpose is accomplished by defining and periodically updating the HR body of knowledge; promoting self-development of HR professionals; and recognizing and credentialing those who have met established experience requirements and have demonstrated mastery of the HR body of knowledge by passing one of the HRCI examinations.

The first certification examinations were administered in the spring of 1976 following years of extensive work by a task force formed by the American Society for Personnel Administration, the forerunner of SHRM. Their efforts resulted in a certification program open to professionals in the HR field.

Today, HRCI is governed by a volunteer board of directors composed of certified HR individuals dedicated to advancing the professionalism in the field. Item writing, item review and examination review panels (also comprised of volunteers) write test questions, review the body of knowledge test specifications and bibliographic reference lists, and review examination forms. HRCI employs a highly qualified staff to administer its certification program.

CERTIFICATION

The Institute offers two levels of certification—Professional in Human Resources (PHR) and Senior Professional in Human Resources (SPHR). To be eligible to take either examination, candidates must have two years of exempt-level HR experience. The PHR examination focuses more on the technical and operational aspects of HR. The SPHR examination focuses more on strategic HR policy issues.

Candidates should select the certification level they feel best represents their mastery of the HR body of knowledge. Candidate performance has shown that appropriate exempt-level HR work experience and educational background contribute significantly to success on the examinations. It is strongly recommended that PHR candidates have two to four years of exempt-level HR experience and that SPHR candidates have six to eight years of exempt-level HR experience. Success depends on mastery of the entire body of knowledge as reflected in the test specifications. Therefore, candidates should carefully assess their qualifications (using the guidelines discussed above) before selecting the certification examination level.

ELIGIBILITY AS A STUDENT OR RECENT GRADUATE

HRCI permits and encourages students to take the PHR certification exam even though they lack the required two years of exempt-level HR experience. To qualify in this category, candidates must not meet the work experience requirements necessary to take the PHR or SPHR examination. Students and recent graduates are permitted to take the exam no earlier than 12 months before their graduation date and recent graduates no later than 12 months after their graduation date. Students/recent graduates have five years from the date of passing the exam to secure the required exempt-level HR work experience. After meeting the experience requirement, students/recent graduates must:

- Provide documentation of graduation;
- Submit documentation outlining the required work experience;
- Pay the balance of the certification fee.

Student/recent graduate candidates who take and pass the examination may not use the PHR designation until they have met the work experience requirement. Candidates qualifying as a student/recent graduate are not eligible to take the SPHR certification examination.

DEFINITIONS

The program established and administered by HRCI is intended for HR professionals who are currently working at an exempt level in the HR field. While that work need not always be exclusively in HR, the majority (51 percent) of a person's daily activities must be within the human resource function. Therefore, the following general definitions apply when assessing eligibility:

Practitioner: One whose duties are those normally found in the typical HR function.

Educator: One whose principal area of instruction is in the HR field in a higher education institution.

Researcher: One whose research activities are restricted primarily to the HR field.

Consultant: One whose consulting activities are predominantly in the HR field.

USE OF CERTIFICATION

HRCI certifications are voluntary in nature and conferred by HRCI solely when a human resource professional has demonstrated achievement of national standards ranging from technical operational knowledge to comprehension of contemporary management concepts and practices. Persons or organizations choosing to incorporate HRCI certification as a condition of employment or advancement do so of their own volition. Candidates must determine for themselves whether the use of such a certification process, including its eligibility and recertification requirements, when coupled with other requirements imposed by such persons, meets their needs and complies with applicable laws.

APPLICATIONS

HRCI annually publishes the *Certification Information Handbook.* This handbook provides information about the certification process and eligibility requirements and includes an application form (not included in the online version). It includes the current examination fee schedule and test center locations. The handbook is available online at www.hrci.org or upon request. To request a hard copy, write, e-mail or phone HRCI:

Human Resource Certification Institute
1800 Duke Street
Alexandria, VA 22314
(703) 548-3440
FAX: (703) 535-6474
TDD: (703) 548-6999
e-mail: info@hrci.org

Candidates should refer only to the most recently issued handbook as HRCI may change or modify policies and procedures from year to year. Similarly, only the most current application form should be used.

RECERTIFICATION

Certification demonstrates mastery of the HR body of knowledge in an increasingly demanding field. As every HR professional knows, however, the field is in constant flux. HR professionals who strive to maintain their professional edge must keep up with the rapid change and new dimensions that define the profession. Recertification is a method for certified professionals to demonstrate that they have stayed abreast of change and updated their knowledge in the HR field.

Recertification is required by HRCI within three years of earning certification. Each subsequent recertification period is also for three years. There are two ways to recertify:

RECERTIFICATION BY EXAMINATION

All requirements for recertification may be met by passing the current, applicable examination. Candidates choosing this option must take the examination before their certification cycle expires. For more information about this method of recertification, please contact HRCI at 1-800-283-7476 opt. 4 or info@hrci.org or visit the HRCI website at www.hrci.org.

RECERTIFICATION BY UPDATING EDUCATION AND EXPERIENCE

Recertification through continuing education and experience can be achieved by accumulating a total of 60 credit/contact hours. Contact hours can be achieved through a variety of methods. Please refer to the latest recertification brochure and application (distributed by HRCI or available at www.hrci.org) for more information on the number of credit hours allowed per category.

Continuing Education: Recertification credit can be earned by participating in HR-related courses, workshops, seminars or conferences. HRCI does not accept recertification credit for attending regularly held association meetings such as those held on a monthly basis. All 60 recertification credit hours can be obtained from this category.

Research and/or Publishing: Recertification credit can be earned by conducting an HR-related research project or by writing and publishing in the HR field. Writing an article for a newsletter will not meet this requirement.

Instruction: Recertification candidates can earn credit hours by preparing for and teaching a new college-level class or making a presentation at a workshop or conference (including in-house training programs). Credits can be earned only for the first time the presentation is made.

One-the-Job: Certain projects at work can earn recertification credit. A first-time work activity that adds to the candidate's HR knowledge base can be credited. The focus in this area is to capture new knowledge.

Leadership: HR professionals can earn recertification credit hours through leadership responsibilities in an HR professional organization such as SHRM at a national, area, state or local level or in a civic/community activity where HR knowledge is the primary reason for the affiliation.

Professional Membership: Recertification credit is awarded at 3 hours a year (up to ten hours maximum) for professionals who are members of a national HR organization such as SHRM.

RECERTIFICATION APPLICATION AND FEES

Application forms for recertification by documentation are available from HRCI and can be downloaded from the HRCI homepage at www.hrci.org. Recertification-by-examination candidates can request a paper form from HRCI at 1-800-283-7476 opt. 4, through the HRCI homepage (www.hrci.org) or by e-mail at info@hrci.org.

SECTION III:

HUMAN RESOURCE BODY OF KNOWLEDGE

DEFINING THE HR BODY OF KNOWLEDGE

What should a human resource practitioner know and be able to apply in order to be considered a competent HR generalist? This is the fundamental question HRCI seeks to answer through its practice analysis study, an extensive ongoing research program specifically designed to define and update the HR body of knowledge.

The HR field is dynamic and in a constant state of change. Consequently, the knowledge requirements must reflect these ever-present changes. The practice analysis process keeps HR knowledge requirements both relevant and up-to-date.

To set standards for the credentialing of a profession, the relevant body of knowledge must first be defined; the HR body of knowledge serves as the foundation upon which HRCI's entire certification program is built. From this body of knowledge, test specifications are developed. In turn, these specifications are used as a blueprint for the certification examinations. Examination items are developed to measure the knowledge requirements that reflect the topics in the test specifications.

The end result of this research is a set of assurances. Assurances that HRCI certifications are:

- Based on a set of well-defined knowledge requirements;
- Current and able to respond to rapid changes in the field;
- Based on "real life" human resource management practices; and
- Focused on important knowledge and not trivial matters.

Codification research, now known as the practice analysis study, began in 1976 with a group of HR experts from throughout the United States. Their roles were to critique draft content outlines and weightings, recommend revisions, suggest sources for bibliographies, and make other pertinent comments.

In 1979, and again in 1984, a modified Delphi technique involving hundreds of professionals was used to revise the content outlines. This method used a multiple nomination technique to identify experts who were widely known and respected as HR leaders. The experts included practitioners, educators, researchers, and consultants. They were asked to perform a highly detailed evaluation of the content outlines and bibliographies. Statistical analyses were performed. The resulting body of knowledge represented the consensus views of those experts.

Before 1988, the codification process methodology used human resource experts for a normative (or what the field ought to be) perspective. In 1988, HRCI, then known as the Personnel Accreditation Institute, with funding supplied by the ASPA Foundation, went to the "real" experts in the HR field for a descriptive (the way it is) perspective. A detailed questionnaire of 234 separate items was mailed to more than 41,000 human resource practitioners, educators, researchers and consultants. Participants were asked to evaluate each of the questions in terms of how essential it was to their particular job. In addition, a number of demographic factors were asked to allow for more in-depth analyses of data.

The data from the questionnaire was reviewed by the HRCI board and SHRM committee chairs. That data was then compiled into a comprehensive content outline that served as the foundation for the 1984 HRCI content outline.

HRCI underwent an equally extensive process in 1997 and 2000 and updated the content outline (now known as test specifications). The new test specifications went into effect on January 1, 2002.

To verify and revise test specifications between major surveys, HRCI uses expert reviews, extensive literature searches, and analyses of HR textbooks. This kind of environmental scan identifies new knowledge requirements and those that may be obsolete. Environmental scans took place in 1992 and 1996.

The current test specifications are the basis for certification testing and for the preparation of these publications/products (this is not an exhaustive list):

- *HRCI® Certification Information Handbook*
- *HRCI® Certification Guide*
- SHRM® Learning System

The HR body of knowledge is constantly changing. Consequently, the Institute's research in this area is ongoing to ensure that the test specifications and examinations reflect current HR knowledge and practices.

HRCI TEST SPECIFICATIONS

HRCI examinations are divided into functional areas. The weighting of each area is based on its relative importance to the knowledge requirements of an HR generalist. The PHR and SPHR examinations are weighted accordingly:

	PHR	SPHR
Strategic Management	12%	26%
Workforce Planning and Employment	26	16
Human Resource Development	15	13
Compensation and Benefits	20	16
Employee and Labor Relations	21	24
Occupational Health, Safety, and Security	6	5

The numbers indicate the percentage composition for each major functional area. The first number is the PHR percentage and the second number is the SPHR percentage.

The numbers in parentheses below indicate the percentage composition for each major functional area. The first number is the PHR percentage and the second number is the SPHR percentage.

STRATEGIC MANAGEMENT (12%, 26%)

The processes and activities used to formulate HR objectives, practices, and policies to meet the short- and long-range organizational needs and opportunities, to guide and lead the change process and to evaluate HR's contributions to organizational effectiveness.

RESPONSIBILITIES:

1. Interpret information related to the organization's operations from internal sources, including financial/accounting, marketing, operations, information technology, and individual employees, in order to participate in strategic planning and policy making.

2. Interpret information related to the general business environment, industry practices and developments, and technological developments from external sources (for example, publications, government documents, media, and trade organizations), in order to participate in strategic planning and policy-making.

3. Participate as a partner in the organization's strategic planning process.

4. Establish strategic relationships with individuals in the organization, to influence organizational decision-making.

5. Establish relationships/alliances with key individuals in the community and in professional capacities to assist in meeting the organization's strategic needs.

6. Evaluate HR's contribution to organizational effectiveness, including assessment, design, implementation, and evaluation of activities with respect to strategic and organizational measurement in HR objectives.

7. Provide direction and guidance during changes in organizational processes, operations, planning, intervention, leadership training and culture that balances the expectations and needs of the organization, its employees, and other stakeholders (including customers).

8. Develop and shape organizational policy related to the organization's management of its human resources.

9. Cultivate leadership and ethical values in self and others through modeling and teaching.

10. Provide information for the organizational budgeting process, including budget development and review.

11. Monitor legislative environment for proposed changes in law and take appropriate action to support, modify, or stop the proposed action (for example, write to a member of Congress, provide expert testimony at a public hearing, lobby legislators).

KNOWLEDGE OF:

1. Lawmaking and administrative regulatory processes.

2. Internal and external environmental scanning techniques.

3. Strategic planning process and implementation.

4. Organizational social responsibility (for example, welfare to work, philanthropy, alliances with community-based organizations).

5. Management functions, including planning, organizing, directing, and controlling.

6. Techniques to sustain creativity and innovation.

WORKFORCE PLANNING AND EMPLOYMENT (26%, 16%)

The processes of planning, developing, implementing, administering, and performing ongoing evaluation of recruiting, hiring, orientation, and organizational exit to ensure that the workforce will meet the organization's goals and objectives.

RESPONSIBILITIES:

1. Identify staffing requirements to meet the goals and objectives of the organization.

2. Conduct job analyses to write job descriptions and develop job competencies.

3. Identify and document the essential job functions for positions.

4. Establish hiring criteria based on the competencies needed.

5. Assess internal workforce, labor market, and recruitment agencies to determine the availability of qualified applicants.

6. Identify internal and external recruitment methods and implement them within the context of the organization's goals and objectives.

7. Develop strategies to market the organization to potential applicants.

8. Establish selection procedures, including interviewing, testing, and reference and background checking.

9. Implement selection procedures, including interviewing, testing, and reference and background checking.

10. Develop and/or extend employment offers.

11. Perform or administer post-offer employment activities (for example, employment agreements, completion of I-9 verification form, relocation agreements, and medical examinations).

12. Facilitate and/or administer the process by which non-US citizens can legally work in the United States.

13. Design, facilitate, and/or conduct the orientation process, including review of performance standards for new hires and transfers.

14. Evaluate selection and employment processes for effectiveness and implement changes if indicated (for example, employee retention).

15. Develop a succession planning process.

16. Develop and implement the organizational exit process, including unemployment insurance claim responses (includes severance, turnover and outplacement).

17. Develop, implement, manage, and evaluate affirmative action program(s), as may be required.

KNOWLEDGE OF:

7. Federal/state/local employment-related laws (for example, Title VII, ADA, ADEA, Vietnam Veterans, WARN) and regulations (for example, EEOC Uniform Guidelines on Employee Selection Procedures).

8. Immigration law (for example, visas, I-9).

9. Quantitative analyses required to assess past and future staffing needs (for example, cost benefit analysis, costs-per-hire, selection ratios, adverse impact).

10. Recruitment methods and sources.

11. Staffing alternatives (for example, telecommuting, outsourcing).

12. Planning techniques (for example, succession planning, forecasting).

13. Reliability and validity of selection tests/tools/methods.

14. Use and interpretation of selection tests (for example, psychological/personality, cognitive, and motor/physical assessments).

15. Interviewing techniques.

16. Relocation practices.

17. Impact of compensation and benefits plans on recruitment and retention.

18. International HR and implications of international workforce for workforce planning and employment.

19. Downsizing and outplacement.

20. Internal workforce planning and employment policies, practices, and procedures.

HUMAN RESOURCE DEVELOPMENT (15%, 13%)

The processes of ensuring that the skills, knowledge, abilities, and performance of the workforce meet the current and future organizational and individual needs through developing, implementing, and evaluating activities and programs addressing employee training and development, change and performance management, and the unique needs of particular employee groups.

RESPONSIBILITIES:

1. Conduct needs analyses to identify and establish priorities regarding human resource development activities.

2. Develop training programs.

3. Implement training programs.

4. Evaluate training programs.

5. Develop programs to assess employees' potential for growth and development in the organization.

6. Implement programs to assess employees' potential for growth and development in the organization.

7. Evaluate programs to assess employees' potential for growth and development in the organization.

8. Develop change management programs and activities.

9. Implement change management programs and activities.

10. Evaluate change management programs and activities.

11. Develop performance management programs and procedures.

12. Implement performance management programs and procedures.

13. Evaluate performance management programs and procedures.

14. Develop programs to meet the unique needs of particular employees (for example, work-family programs, diversity programs, outplacement programs, repatriation programs, and fast-track programs).

15. Implement programs to meet the unique needs of particular employees (for example, work-family programs, diversity programs, outplacement programs, repatriation programs, and fast-track programs).

16. Evaluate programs to meet the unique needs of particular employees (for example, work-family programs, diversity programs, outplacement programs, repatriation programs, and fast-track programs).

KNOWLEDGE OF:

21. Applicable international, federal, state, and local laws and regulations regarding copyrights and patents.

22. Human resource development theories and applications (including career development and leadership development).

23. Organizational development theories and applications.

24. Training methods, programs, and techniques (design, objectives, methods, etc.).

25. Employee involvement strategies.

26. Task/process analysis.

27. Performance appraisal and performance management methods.

28. Applicable international issues (for example, culture, local management approaches/practices, societal norms).

29. Instructional methods and program delivery (content, building modules of program, selection of presentation/delivery mechanism).

30. Techniques to assess HRD program effectiveness (for example, satisfaction, learning and job performance of program participants, and organizational outcomes such as turnover and productivity).

COMPENSATION AND BENEFITS (20%, 16%)

The processes of analyzing, developing, implementing, administering, and performing ongoing evaluation of a total compensation and benefits system for all employee groups consistent with human resource management goals.

RESPONSIBILITIES:

1. Ensure the compliance of compensation and benefits with applicable federal, state, and local laws. (includes IRS rulings).

2. Analyze, develop, implement, and maintain compensation policies and a pay structure consistent with the organization's strategic objectives (includes broad definitions and designs).

3. Analyze and evaluate pay rates based on internal worth and external market conditions (includes wage and salary surveys).

4. Develop/select and implement a payroll system.

5. Administer payroll functions.

6. Evaluate compensation policies to ensure that they are positioning the organization internally and externally according to the organization's strategic objectives.

7. Conduct a benefit plan needs assessment and determine/select the plans to be offered, considering the organization's strategic objectives.

8. Implement and administer benefit plans (addresses more the carrying out the objectives of the benefit plan).

9. Evaluate benefits program to ensure that it is positioning the organization internally and externally according to the organization's strategic objectives.

10. Analyze, select, implement, maintain, and administer executive compensation, stock purchase, stock options, and incentive, and bonus programs. (includes profit-sharing).

11. Analyze, develop, select, maintain, and implement expatriate and foreign national compensation and benefit programs.

12. Communicate the compensation and benefits plan and policies to the workforce.

KNOWLEDGE OF:

31. Federal, state, and local compensation and benefit laws (for example, FLSA, ERISA, COBRA).

32. Accounting practices related to compensation and benefits (for example, excess group term life, compensatory time).

33. Job evaluation methods.

34. Job pricing and pay structures.

35. Incentive and variable pay methods.

36. Executive compensation.

37. Non-cash compensation methods (for example, stock option plans).

38. Benefits needs analysis.

39. Benefit plans (for example, health insurance, life insurance, pension, education, health club).

40. International compensation laws and practices (for example, expatriate compensation, socialized medicine, mandated retirement).

EMPLOYEE AND LABOR RELATIONS (21%, 24%)

The processes of analyzing, developing, implementing, administering, and performing ongoing evaluation of the workplace relationship between employer and employee (including the collective bargaining process and union relations), in order to maintain effective relationships and working conditions that balance the employer's needs with the employees' rights in support of the organization's strategic objectives.

RESPONSIBILITIES:

1. Ensure compliance with all applicable federal, state, and local laws and regulations (catch-all responsibility, including NLRB, ADA, FMLA).

2. Develop and implement employee relations programs that will create a positive organizational culture (most of the legal definitions and general definitions).

3. Promote, monitor, and measure the effectiveness of employee relations activities.

4. Assist in establishing work rules and monitor their application and enforcement to ensure fairness and consistency (for union and non-union environments).

5. Communicate and ensure understanding by employees of laws, regulations, and organizational policies.

6. Resolve employee complaints filed with federal, state, and local agencies involving employment practices (formal, legal complaints).

7. Develop grievance and disciplinary policies and procedures to ensure fairness and consistency.

8. Implement and monitor grievance and disciplinary policies and procedures to ensure fairness and consistency (includes investigation).

9. Respond to union organizing activity.

10. Participate in collective bargaining activities, including contract negotiation and administration.

KNOWLEDGE OF:

41. Applicable federal, state, and local laws affecting employment in union and non-union environments, such as anti-discrimination laws, sexual harassment, labor relations, and privacy.

42. Techniques for facilitating positive employee relations (for example, small group facilitation, dispute resolution, and labor/management cooperative strategies and programs).

43. Employee involvement strategies (for example, alternate work schedules, work teams).

44. Individual employment rights issues and practices (for example, employment-at-will, negligent hiring, defamation, employees' rights to bargain collectively).

45. Workplace behavior issues/practices (for example, absenteeism, discipline).

46. Methods for assessment of employee attitudes, opinions, and satisfaction (for example, opinion surveys, attitude surveys, focus panels).

47. Unfair labor practices.

48. The collective bargaining process, strategies, and concepts (up to and after contract).

49. Public sector labor relations issues and practices.

50. Expatriation and repatriation issues and practices.

51. Employee and labor relations for local nationals (i.e., labor relations in other countries).

OCCUPATIONAL HEALTH, SAFETY, AND SECURITY (6%, 5%)

The processes of analyzing, developing, implementing, administering, and performing ongoing evaluation of programs, practices, and services to promote the physical and mental well-being of individuals in the workplace, and to protect individuals and the workplace from unsafe acts, unsafe working conditions, and violence.

RESPONSIBILITIES:

1. Ensure compliance with all applicable federal, state, and local workplace health and safety laws and regulations.

2. Determine safety programs needed for the organization.

3. Develop and/or select injury/occupational illness prevention programs.

4.   Implement injury/occupational illness prevention programs.

5.   Develop and/or select safety training and incentive programs.

6.   Implement safety training and incentive programs.

7.   Evaluate the effectiveness of safety prevention, training, and incentive programs.

8.   Implement workplace injury/occupational illness procedures (for example, workers' compensation, OSHA).

9.   Determine health and wellness programs needed for the organization.

10. Develop/select, implement, and evaluate (or make available) health and wellness programs.

11. Develop/select, implement, and evaluate security plans to protect the company from liability.

12. Develop/select, implement, and evaluate security plans to protect employees (for example, injuries resulting from workplace violence).

13. Develop/select, implement, and evaluate incident and emergency response plans (for example, natural disasters, workplace safety threats, evacuation).

KNOWLEDGE OF:

52. Federal, state, and local workplace health and safety laws and regulations (for example, OSHA, Drug-Free Workplace Act, ADA).

53. Workplace injury and occupational illness compensation laws and programs (for example, workers' compensation).

54. Investigation procedures of workplace safety, health, and security enforcement agencies (for example, OSHA).

55. Workplace safety risks.

56. Workplace security risks (for example, theft, corporate espionage, information systems/technology, and vandalism).

57. Potential violent behavior and workplace violence conditions.

58. General health and safety practices (for example, fire evacuation, HAZCOM, ergonomic evaluations).

59. Incident and emergency response plans.

60. Internal investigation and surveillance techniques.

61. Employee Assistance Programs.

62. Employee wellness programs.

63. Issues related to chemical use and dependency (for example, identification of symptoms, drug testing, discipline).

CORE KNOWLEDGE REQUIRED BY HR PROFESSIONALS

64. Needs assessment and analysis.

65. Third-party contract management, including development of requests for proposals (RFPs).

66. Communication strategies.

67. Documentation requirements.

68. Adult learning processes.

69. Motivation concepts and applications.

70. Training methods.

71. Leadership concepts and applications.

72. Project management concepts and applications.

73. Diversity concepts and applications.

74. Human relations concepts and applications (for example, interpersonal and organizational behavior).

75. HR ethics and professional standards.

76. Technology and human resource information systems (HRIS) to support HR activities.

77. Qualitative and quantitative methods and tools for analysis, interpretation, and decision-making purposes.

78. Change management.

79. Liability and risk management.

80. Job analysis and job description methods.

81. Employee records management (for example, retention, disposal).

82. The interrelationships among HR activities and programs across functional areas.

RESOURCES

These selected resources, categorized by the functional areas of the examination, may help you prepare for the Institute's certification examination. No attempt has been made to provide an inclusive list of resources. These resources represent a solid foundation for a human resource professional library.

STRATEGIC MANAGEMENT

Anthony, William, Pamela Perrewe and K. Michele Kacmar, *Strategic Human Resource Management*, 3rd ed, The Dryden Press, 1998.

Baird, Lloyd S., *Managing Human Resources: Integrating People and Business Strategy*, Irwin Professional Publishing, 1992.

Bernarding, H. John, *Human Resources Management: An Experimental Approach*, McGraw-Hill Companies, 1997.

Carrell, Michael R., Norbert F. Elbert and Robert D. Hatfield, *Human Resource Management: Strategies for Managing a Diverse and Global Workforce*, The Dryden Press, 2000.

Cascio, Wayne F., *Costing Human Resources: The Financial Impact of Behavior in Organizations*, 4th ed., Kent Publishing Company, 1999.

Cascio, Wayne F., *Managing Human Resources*, 6th ed., McGraw-Hill Companies, 2001.

DeCenzo, David A. and Stephen P. Robbins, *Human Resource Management: Concepts and Practices*, 6th ed., John Wiley & Sons, Inc., 1999.

Dessler, Gary, *Essentials of Human Resource Management*, 1st ed., Prentice Hall, Inc., 1999.

Dowling, Peter J., Randall S. Schuler and Denice E. Welch, *International Dimensions of Human Resource Management*, 3rd ed., Wadsworth Publishing Company, 1998.

Ferris, Gerald R. and M. Ronald Buckley, eds., *Human Resource Management: Perspectives, Context, Functions, and Outcomes*, 3rd ed., Prentice Hall, Inc., 1995.

Gomez-Mejia, Luis R., David B. Balkin and Robert L. Cardy, *Managing Human Resources*, 2nd ed., Prentice Hall, 1999.

Harvey, Don and Robert B. Bowin, *Human Resource Management: An Experimental Approach*, 2nd ed, Prentice Hall, 2000.

International HR Learning System, Society for Human Resource Management, 2002.

Ivancevich, John M., *Human Resource Management*, 6th ed., Homewood, IL: Richard D. Irwin, Inc., 2000.

Lewin, David and Daniel J. Mitchel, *Human Resource Management: An Economic Approach*, 2nd ed., South-Western Publishing Company, 1994.

Mathis, Robert L. and John H. Jackson, *Human Resource Management*, 9th ed., West Publishing Company, 2000.

Miner, John B. and Donald P. Crane, *Human Resource Management: The Strategic Perspective*, Addison-Wesley Publishing Co., 1995.

Schuler, Randall S., *Managing Human Resources in the Information Age*, 5th ed., West Wadsworth Press, 1994.

Schuler, Randall S., *Strategic Human Resource Management*, Blackwell Publishing, 1999.

Sherman, Arthur W., Jr. and George W. Bohlander, *Managing Human Resources*, 12th ed, South-Western Publishing Company, 2000.

SHRM Learning System, Society for Human Resource Management, 2002.

Sisson, Keith, *Personnel Management: A Comprehensive Guide to Theory and Practice*, 2nd ed., Blackwell Publishers, 2000.

Torrington, Derek and Laura Hall, *Personnel Management: HRM in Action*, 3rd ed., Englewood Cliffs, NJ: Prentice Hall, Inc., 1995.

WORKFORCE PLANNING AND EMPLOYMENT

Fitz-Enz, Jac, *The ROI of Human Capital: Measuring the Economic Value of Employee Performance*, AMACOM, 2000.

Gatewood, Robert D. and Hubert S. Feild, *Human Resource Selection*, 4th ed., The Dryden Press, 1997.

Schmitt, Neal and Walter C. Borman and Associates, *Personnel Selection in Organizations*, Jossey-Bass, Inc., 1992.

HUMAN RESOURCE DEVELOPMENT

Schneier, Craig Eric and Craig J. Russell, Richard W. Beatty and Lloyd S. Baird, *Training and Development Sourcebook*, 2nd ed., Human Resource Development Press, 1993.

Tracey, William R., *Human Resources Management and Development Handbook*, 2nd ed., AMACOM, 1994.

COMPENSATION AND BENEFITS

Henderson, Richard I., *Compensation Management: In a Knowledge-Based World*, 8th ed, Prentice Hall, 1999.

Heneman, Robert L., *Business-Driven Compensation Policies: Integrating Compensation Systems with Corporate Strategies*, AMACOM, 2000.

Lawler, Edward E., III, *Strategic Pay: Aligning Organizational Strategies and Pay Systems*, Jossey-Bass, Inc., 1990.

EMPLOYEE AND LABOR RELATIONS

BNA Editorial Staff, *Grievance Guide*, 10th ed., BNA Books, 2000.

Ballot, Michael; Laurie Lichter-Heath; Thomas Kail; Ruth Want. *Labor-Management Relations in a Changing Environment*, John Wiley & Sons, 1995.

Carrell, Michael and Christina Heavrin, *Labor Relations and Collective Bargaining Cases*, Practices and Law, Prentice Hall, 2000.

OCCUPATIONAL HEALTH, SAFETY AND SECURITY

Blosser, Fred, *Primer on Occupational Safety and Health*, The Bureau of National Affairs, Inc., 1992.

Diberardinis, Louis J., *Handbook of Occupational Safety and Health*. Wiley-Interscience, 1998.

SECTION IV:

HRCI CERTIFICATION EXAMINATIONS

CERTIFICATION EXAMINATIONS

The Institute's PHR and SPHR certification examinations are administered twice a year throughout the United States in more than 95 test centers. Both examinations consist of 225 multiple-choice questions, each with four possible answers. Of the 225 questions, 25 are pre-test questions not counted in the scoring of the exam but used for statistical purposes. Four hours are allotted to complete the examination. A passing (or cut) score is determined using the expert judgments of a standards setting panel. This score will vary depending on the actual examination form used.

The examinations measure mastery of the body of knowledge. Both examination levels cover the same functional areas but differ in terms of the individual test items and the functional area's percentile weightings. Preparation for the examination is best accomplished by mastering the application of the human resource (HR) body of knowledge.

The certification examinations are made up of four-option multiple-choice items because they:

- Are flexible and adaptable.
- Tend to be more reliable than other formats.
- Can accommodate a wide range of skills, knowledge and abilities to be measured.
- Provide a good sampling.
- Have low chance scores.
- Can be machine scored.

Multiple-choice items consist of three parts:

STEM

The stem states the problem or question to be answered.

CORRECT ANSWER

The correct answer is one of four potential options that represent the only correct response or best correct response. "Best" means a panel of experts would agree to this judgment.

DISTRACTORS

The remaining options are distractors and are incorrect responses. They are plausible, yet wrong or not the best possible answer.

The following is an example of the parts of a multiple-choice item:

STEM: Typically, the most unreliable tool utilized in the selection process is a(n)

       Correct Answer: A. employment interview.
       Distractor: B. selection test.
       Distractor: C. physical examination.
       Distractor: D. background check.

Certified HR professionals write all examination questions. These important volunteers serve on one of two HRCI Item Writing Panels and are given extensive training and specific guidelines on item development.

Once written, examination questions (known as items) go through an exhaustive item review process. A separate group of certified HR professionals (Item Review Panels) thoroughly scrutinize each item and perform a number of validity checks. Each remaining item is then categorized as either a PHR or SPHR item and coded to the Institute's test specifications.

A third group of HR professionals—the Examination Review Panel—reviews and certifies each examination form before use.

This three-step process of item development, item review and examination review assures that items are:

- Clear, unambiguous and grammatically proper.
- Technically correct.
- Appropriate in terms of fairness—geographically, ethnically or culturally.
- Important for HR professionals to know.
- Correctly coded to the HRCI content outline.

The PHR and SPHR examinations differ significantly in terms of the weights assigned to each of the functional areas. Of equal importance is the difference in focus and format of the individual items on the examinations. In general, PHR items are more technical application questions. Many are at the operational level. On the other hand, SPHR items tend to be more policy application questions. Many are at the strategic level. Additionally, there are a greater proportion of scenario questions on the SPHR examination. A scenario question poses an HR situation followed by a series of questions based on the information supplied. Scenario questions are particularly well suited to SPHR examinees because they represent typical situations that senior-level HR practitioners encounter and the diverse knowledge requirements needed to solve those situations.

Examinations are administered through a professional testing service. This organization supplies expert counsel in examination design, construction, and administration and also provides analysis of examination results.

EXAMINATION PREPARATION METHODS, STRATEGIES, AND RESOURCES

Exam preparation is an important issue for candidates. There are a number of study methods available for the examinations; selecting a method is a matter of individual preference based on what best fits into one's lifestyle. Methods range from the highly informal individual self-study to highly structured courses and workshops.

The strategy to prepare for a certification examination is equally important. Just like world class athletes must peak at the precise moment of competition, so must candidates on examination day. In addition to being able to master the HR body of knowledge, candidates should be both mentally and physically prepared to take the examination. Strategy is a critical element of preparation.

Study resources are also critical elements of preparation. Sometimes the resources will be a function of the preparation method selected. Other times, candidates will have to choose resources from a wide range of possibilities. A mistake in selecting resources can significantly affect test scores.

Choose a study method carefully. Because the examinations measure mastery of the application of the HR body of knowledge, it is impossible to train or teach to the examination. Instead, knowing the HR knowledge requirements and how to apply them are the best preparation. Study methods based on the actual examinations' format are preferable because they familiarize test takers with the Institute's test specifications.

HRCI is a standard-setting and credentialing organization. As such, it does not provide professional development activities or endorse any particular study method. The Society for Human Resource Management's professional development department, however, may be a resource in surveying and selecting a preparation method.

EXAMINATION PREPARATION METHODS

Self-Study

Self-study can either be individual, where candidates study at their own pace and on their own schedules or it can be a group experience where there are regular meetings, mutual assistance and lively exchanges of ideas and information among members. The key concept to self-study programs, whether individual or group-based, is flexibility.

Individual self-study requires a high degree of personal discipline. Candidates who choose this method must develop study strategies, prepare schedules, and be committed to abide by those schedules. Prepackaged preparation systems such as the *SHRM® Learning System* are convenient for this purpose. Also, any of the general HR references cited in this book can be used as a starting point for individual self-study.

A modified version of individual self-study is paired self-study. This method uses the buddy system, where two candidates pair together and use the same format as with individual self-study. It is highly flexible, yet at the same time gives candidates a support system.

Group Study

Group study offers some advantages over individual and paired self-study. The camaraderie and group support can be a great asset. Many SHRM chapters sponsor certification study groups.

Key concepts to consider when forming a study group:

- Establish convenient meeting locations and times.
- Secure a certified HR professional to serve as a mentor to the group.
- Use pre-and post-tests using an examination similar to the one used in this guide.
- Design a study format with a schedule and individual member assignments.
- Use multiple resources for preparation.

When flexibility is important, self-study methods, whether individual, paired, or group are potential ways to study for the examination.

College and University Courses

Many colleges and universities offer study courses to prepare for the examinations. Most often these courses are offered on a non-credit/continuing education basis; some academic institutions, however, grant credit for these courses.

A number of colleges and universities have partnered with SHRM to offer a certification preparation course using the *SHRM® Learning System*, a study program that was developed using HRCI test specifications as a blue print. Other colleges and universities use other materials.

Quality of instruction and resources should be carefully scrutinized and it is always advisable to check references with past course participants before registering for such courses.

SHRM Chapter-Sponsored Short Courses

Many local SHRM chapters offer short courses to study for the HRCI examinations. These short courses provide instruction and a structured program that cover the HRCI body of knowledge. Local SHRM chapters should be contacted to determine availability of these courses in your area (for a list of SHRM chapters, visit the SHRM web page at www.shrm.org).

SHRM Certification Preparation Course

Candidates with a good understanding of the HR field may be interested in the SHRM Review Course for Certification. This course is an intensive refresher or review of the HR body of knowledge and is designed for experienced HR practitioners who need a refresher before the examination. It is offered nationally in selected locations before each of HRCI's national examination dates. Information about this course can be obtained by calling the SHRM professional development department at 1-800-283-7476 or by visiting the SHRM web page at www.shrm.org.

Private Training Organizations

Some private training organizations now offer courses to prepare for the HRCI examinations. Candidates should be sure that the approach used in the course corresponds to the HRCI test specifications.

If the certification method employs instructors, it is important that they be certified. It is hard—if not impossible—to teach about an examination one has not taken. Personal experiences of instructors offer valuable insights and increase the comfort levels of examinees.

Regardless of the method, a high degree of personal commitment is needed to receive the most benefit from the preparation experience.

STRATEGIES

Any preparation method must have a strategy to maximize self-assessment, structure time, build mental and physical preparedness and address post-examination emotions.

Self-Assassment

No two candidates bring the same education, experience and preparation to the table. As a result, it is important to conduct an honest self-assessment of your qualifications and HR work experience.

Begin by reviewing your education and work experience in light of the test specifications. Compare your resume side-by-side with the test specifications. In what areas have education and experience given you a strong knowledge and application base? What will you have to work on? Make a list of your strengths and weaknesses.

Next, take the practice examination in this book, resisting the temptation to look at the answers before completing the test. Correct the test and total your score in each of the functional areas of the examination. Is there a correlation between the test results and the self-assessment? Keep in mind that the practice examination is only 125 questions; there are 200 scorable questions in the actual examination. Even though the practice examination is shorter, it is still an important assessment tool.

This kind of self-assessment will help candidates center on those areas where the most preparation is needed. Always focus on the areas where you need the most preparation based upon the weightings of the specific examination (PHR or SPHR) you will take.

Structuring Time

Once the self-assessment is completed, map a formal approach in how you will spend your time to study for the test. Structuring time will be different depending on the level of examination (PHR or SPHR) and the self-assessment. The following are sample 8, 9 and 10-week study schedules:

EIGHT WEEK SCHEDULE

PHR Examination

Week	Topic
1	Introduction and Pre-test
2	Strategic Management
3	Workforce Planning and Employment
4	Human Resource Development
5	Compensation and Benefits
6	Compensation and Benefits; Employee and Labor Relations
7	Employee and Labor Relations
8	Occupational Health, Safety and Security; Post-test

SPHR Examination

Week	Topic
1	Introduction and Pre-test
2	Strategic Management
3	Strategic Management
4	Workforce Planning and Employment
5	Human Resource Development
6	Compensation and Benefits
7	Employee and Labor Relations
8	Occupational Health, Safety and Security; Post-test

TEN WEEK SCHEDULE

PHR Examination

Week	Topic
1	Introduction and Pre-test
2	Strategic Management
3	Workforce Planning and Employment
4	Workforce Planning and Employment
5	Human Resource Development
6	Compensation and Benefits
7	Compensation and Benefits
8	Employee and Labor Relations
9	Employee and Labor Relations
10	Occupational Health, Safety and Security; Post-test

SPHR Examination

Week	Topic
1	Introduction and Pre-test
2	Strategic Management
3	Strategic Management
4	Workforce Planning and Employment
5	Workforce Planning and Employment; Human Resource Development
6	Human Resource Development; Compensation and Benefits

7	Compensation and Benefits
8	Employee and Labor Relations
9	Employee and Labor Relations
10	Occupational Health, Safety and Security; Post-test

TWELVE WEEK SCHEDULE

PHR Examination

Week	Topic
1	Introduction and Pre-test
2	Strategic Management
3	Strategic Management
4	Workforce Planning and Placement
5	Workforce Planning and Placement
6	Workforce Planning and Placement/Human Resource Development
7	Human Resource Development
8	Compensation and Benefits
9	Compensation and Benefits
10	Employee and Labor Relations
11	Employee and Labor Relations
12	Occupational Health, Safety and Security; Post-test

SPHR Examination

Week	Topic
1	Introduction and Pre-test
2	Strategic Management
3	Strategic Management
4	Strategic Management
5	Workforce Planning and Placement
6	Workforce Planning and Placement
7	Human Resource Development
8	Compensation and Benefits
9	Compensation and Benefits
10	Employee and Labor Relations
11	Employee and Labor Relations
12	Occupational Health, Safety and Security; Post-Test

Customize these sample schedules based on your self-assessment, keeping in mind that preparation time is directly related to examination performance.

Mental and Physical Preparedness

Cramming the week or night before the examination is a common mistake made by many examinees. In reality, such behavior hurts examination performance. Preparation is best if spaced over an extended period of time.

Given the nature of examinations, a clear head will help performance more than any limited knowledge gained by last minute cramming. HRCI examinations are intellectually challenging and fatiguing; arriving at a test site already tired from cramming the night before is not a wise strategy. Prepare early and relax the night before the examination. Go out to eat or to a movie the night before, get a good night's rest, and come to the testing center relaxed and alert.

Post-Examination Emotions

It is important to acknowledge and prepare for post-examination emotions. The two emotions that are most likely to occur after taking the test are both frustration-related. First, candidates report feeling frustrated because they do not know how they performed on the examination. Second, they feel frustrated because they do not know what they could have done to perform any better. Both of these emotions are quite common for any examination that assesses mastery in a particular field.

Unlike curriculum-based tests, these examinations cannot be "taught to". Realize that these feelings of frustration are common, recognize them and be prepared to address them after the examination.

Resources

Some preparation methods, such as university or college courses, will provide or identify the resources to be used in the class. Other preparation methods leave it up to the prospective examinee. Therefore, choosing the appropriate resources is critically important.

Because the examinations measure mastery of the entire HR body of knowledge, there is no one best resource to use to study for the exam.

To understand the importance of using a variety of resources, imagine a giant globe filled with marbles. Each marble represents one piece of the HR body of knowledge from each of the functional areas. Each level of the examination is composed of a random drawing of marbles according to the percentage listed for each functional area in the test specifications.

If you can visualize the giant globe filled with thousands of marbles, you can easily see that it is impossible to predict which of the marbles will end up on the exam. It is equally impossible for any one preparatory resource to contain all the marbles. This is why HRCI recommends using a variety of resources for the most comprehensive exposure to the test specifications.

The Institute's mission is to identify the HR body of knowledge and to develop test specifications to measure mastery of this knowledge. It does not develop the resources to teach the test specifications or to test a candidate's mastery of those resources. To maintain examination integrity, HRCI separates itself from the development of preparatory resources and does not endorse any particular resource. Below, though, is a partial list of resources available. For a more complete list of resources, please refer to the resources in Section III of this guide.

The *SHRM® Learning System* covers all functional areas of the test specifications and includes self-directed modules, application activities and end-of-module examinations. It was designed to follow the HRCI test specifications and is available from SHRM.

HR textbooks are a good resource. Be sure to select textbooks that are up-to-date, since the HR field changes rapidly. Textbooks published more than one or two years ago should be used with great caution. It is also recommended that several texts be used, rather than just one, so that candidates see different perspectives.

Custom-designed resources are used by some SHRM chapters and proprietary companies. Many of these resources are not original works but are committee-assembled compilations of other resources

Lending libraries are popular with some SHRM chapters. Learning resources are purchased and made available to chapter members at no cost or for a nominal fee. This allows members to review materials they may not otherwise be able to afford.

EXAMINATION-TAKING SKILLS

It is natural to have some anxieties and nervousness about taking an examination; the anxiety level is likely to be even greater for candidates who have been out of school for several years.

All of the questions on the HRCI examinations are multiple-choice. The question statement is called the stem and the answers are called choices. Some of the choices are designed to be plausible but incorrect, and they are called distractors.

Questions on the exam are of different types, especially at the PHR level. Some will be identification questions, which means that definitions of concepts or facts are being assessed. Relationship questions are used to test how one concept is related to or affects another one. Other questions are application in nature; a situation is posed and the choices reflect applying certain facts to the situation

Below are some test-taking suggestions to help candidates perform up to their capabilities and knowledge.

1. **Mark on the test booklet.** The test booklet is for your use. Feel free to mark on it by making notes, doing simple calculations, placing an x by implausible answers, and putting question marks by questions you do not answer the first time through the exam. You will be asked to return the test booklet with your completed examination.

2. **Trust your first impression.** There is a correct answer to each question. It is widely believed that your first impression of the correct answer will be a better choice.

3. **Avoid over-analyzing.** Be careful not to read too much into an answer.

4. **If uncertain, leave the answer blank and return to it later.** If you cannot decide on an answer, mark the question in the margin of the examination booklet and return to it after answering all of the questions on the exam. It is possible that later questions may trigger information useful for those "undecided" questions.

5. **Don't stop.** If you are stumped by a question, continue to the next one. Otherwise, you may lose valuable time.

6. **Don't look for answer patterns.** The psychometric testing process used by HRCI ensures that questions do not fall into patterns. Contrary to some myths, "c" is not necessarily the most frequent answer and the first answer may be correct.

7. **The length of an answer is a false clue.** It is a myth that the longer an answer, the more likely it is to be correct. However, it often is more difficult to write incorrect distractors than the correct answer, so it is just as likely that the longest answer is incorrect as it is correct.

8. **Eliminate obvious distractors.** For most questions, there are two distractors that usually appear to be incorrect; one that is likely to be plausible but incorrect; and one correct answer. When you first read a question, you should be able to eliminate two of the answers as incorrect. If you cannot decide between the other two, move on to the next question and return to the unanswered question later.

9. **Try to identify the answer before reading the choices.** After reading the question, try to answer the question before reading the choices. By doing this, you will more likely have one answer stand out as being correct.

10. **Use "educated guesses".** If you still cannot decide on a correct answer after eliminating one or two choices, choose one anyway. There is no penalty for guessing on the exam.

11. **Don't worry about what you don't know.** If you don't know the answer to a question, don't fret about it and let it affect your outlook when answering other questions.

12. **Review your answers.** After going through all the questions on the exam, go back and answer the questions left unanswered the first time. Also, be sure that you answered all questions and that you marked the appropriate answers to each question.

13. **Don't rush.** There are no points for finishing first. Use the time allotted to review and check your answers. Keep in mind that someone who finishes early may know less than you do, so don't feel self-conscious about being among the last to turn in your exam.

14. **Don't worry after the test.** Many people feel drained and inadequate after taking a long exam. That feeling is not necessarily directly related to doing poorly on the exam.

PRACTICE EXAMINATION, ANSWERS, RATIONALES & CODING

These practice items are designed to familiarize candidates with the style and format of HRCI examination questions. This practice test is shorter than the actual examinations (it has 125 practice items versus 200 scoreable questions on the actual exam). None of these items will be found on the HRCI examinations, but are representative of the types of questions found in them. To help you in your self-assessment, a scoring sheet and the rationale for the answers follow these practice item. The answers include how the items are coded according to the HRCI content outline.

Remember to select the BEST answer. Good luck!

1. For which position would an employer most likely be able to support a BFOQ based upon sex?

   a. Sportscaster.
   b. Locker room attendant.
   c. Nurse.
   d. OB-GYN physician.

2. Which of the following positions is considered an HR specialist?

   a. Industrial Relations Director.
   b. Human Resource Manager.
   c. Personnel Administrator.
   d. Human Resource Team Leader.

3. In conducting a cost/benefit analysis of a training program, costs are often broken down into direct and indirect costs. Which of the following represents an indirect cost?

   a. Participants' salary.
   b. Training department's overhead.
   c. Training materials.
   d. Trainer's salary.

4. What restriction is placed on NLRB certification of a unit of security guards?

    a. The same restrictions as in units of other employees.
    b. The union seeking certification must represent only guards.
    c. The expiration date of the guards contract cannot coincide with that of the plant union.
    d. The union must include all plant employees.

5. An expatriate's expenses for home travel are deductible for U.S. tax purposes if the trip is made to:

    a. the U.S.
    b. the principal residence in the U.S.
    c. anywhere outside of the country of assignment.
    d. the location of the last employment in the U.S.

6. Which of the following is the best predictor of future performance?

    a. Past performance.
    b. Psychological tests.
    c. Present supervisor assessment.
    d. Former supervisor assessment.

7. Which type of data is generally unavailable to an HR manager in evaluating the effectiveness of an external Employee Assistance Program?

    a. Initial diagnosis category.
    b. Referral source.
    c. Vitalization percent.
    d. Treatment outcome.

8. What is the most effective form of upward communication?

    a. Suggestion systems.
    b. Employee petitions.
    c. Grievance procedures.
    d. Direct discussions between supervisors and employees.

9. In which of the following content areas is it most difficult to evaluate the effectiveness of training?

    a. Typing skills.
    b. Human relations.
    c. Accident reduction.
    d. Grievance reduction.

10. Which of the following questions asked during an interview would most likely give rise to an inference of discrimination?

    a. Describe your military experience.
    b. Do you have a job-related disability?
    c. To what professional organizations do you belong?
    d. Describe the extracurricular activities you did in college.

11. In order for a union to prevail during a representation election, it must win:

    a. a majority of the votes cast in an election.
    b. 51% of the votes of those eligible to vote in the election.
    c. two-thirds of the votes cast in the election.
    d. 30% of the votes cast.

12. When conducting an environmental scan, supply and demand for specific skills, changes in competitors' practices, and unemployment levels are all examples of which of the following influences?

    a. Geographic.
    b. Governmental.
    c. Labor market.
    d. Union.

13. To ensure that a job-training program is valid, a trainer will emphasize:

    a. conducting a job/task analysis.
    b. observing and interviewing the most productive incumbents in a job.
    c. surveying what programs are commercially available in the specific job area.
    d. outlining the traits necessary to perform the job.

14. How do employees tend to perceive the pay of their peers and supervisors when they do not know what the actual pay is?

    a. They overestimate the pay of both their peers and their supervisors.
    b. They underestimate the pay of both their peers and their supervisors.
    c. They underestimate the pay of their peers and overestimate that of their supervisors.
    d. They overestimate the pay of their peers and underestimate that of their supervisors.

15. At the beginning of a given year, a shipping department has four people, each paid $1,000 per month. In that year, each of these employees receives a pay raise of $100 per month. The raises are given January 1, March 1, July 1 and November 1, respectively. The salary increases increase the payroll cost for the year by:

    a. 6.25%.
    b. 7%.
    c. 9%.
    d. 10%.

16. In order to avoid a charge of negligent hiring, an employer should give special attention to which phase of a selection system?

    a. Interviewing.
    b. Honesty testing.
    c. Reference checking.
    d. Medical examinations.

17. All employers with _____ or more employees, must file an annual EEO-I (or I-VI) with the EEOC.

    a. 15.
    b. 20.
    c. 50.
    d. 100.

18. The most difficult problem in forecasting demand for employees is:

   a. forecasting internal supply.
   b. estimating turnover patterns.
   c. determining the supply of human resources.
   d. determining the relationship between personnel demand and the firm's output.

19. In order to prevail in a charge of discrimination based upon selecting participants for a training program, it is most appropriate for the organization to:

   a. establish a quota system to insure minority representation.
   b. ensure the selection of trainees is well documented and does not result in adverse impact.
   c. utilize a self-nomination method of selecting participants.
   d. use diversity training as the initial phase of the training program.

20. The proportion of a sales representative's income that is incentive pay should be relatively large when:

   a. the company does not do much advertising.
   b. customer service is a major consideration.
   c. the product is superior to its competition.
   d. the nature of the product requires team selling.

21. Which of the following is the best process for validating an employment application form as a selection device?

   a. Correlating responses to test scores.
   b. Determining if the information reported on the application is correct.
   c. Examining each item and determining to what extent it helped to predict job success.
   d. Receiving approval from top management for its use in selection of applicants.

22. The primary advantage of a computerized internal skills inventory is that:

    a. it permits employers to predict which additional skills are needed for the workforce of the future.
    b. managers have access to much more sensitive information than in manual systems.
    c. EEOC guidelines recommend automated systems.
    d. job candidates have more confidence in systems that minimize the possibility of personal bias.

23. Which type of psychological test measures an individual's overall ability to learn?

    a. Aptitude.
    b. Interest.
    c. Personality.
    d. Specific abilities.

24. Which of the following may legally be stated in an organization's employee relations policy?

    a. Increase pay for remaining non-union.
    b. Plant closure if unionized.
    c. Organizational opposition to unions.
    d. Endorsement of a specific union.

25. What is the primary purpose of a flexible benefit plan?

    a. Allow employees to contribute pretax dollars to buy additional benefits.
    b. Continuously update benefit options as employees needs and desires change.
    c. Pass along benefit premium increases to employees.
    d. Combine all time-off benefits into a pool from which an employee can take off with pay.

26. For effective learning to occur, the amount of information, its complexity and its rate of presentation should be directed to:

    a. fall within perceptual and comprehension spans of the learners.
    b. accommodate the organizational culture in which the learners exist.
    c. fall within the levels with which the instructors teaching the material are comfortable.
    d. accommodate post-training practices felt most desirable by employee's line management.

27. Assuming no willful violation, what is the statute of limitations for recovery of back pay under the Fair Labor Standards Act?

    a. 2 years.
    b. 3 years.
    c. 4 years.
    d. 5 years.

28. During a unionization drive, which of the following may a supervisor legally do?

    a. Visit the homes of employees for the purpose of urging them to reject the union.
    b. Inform the employees that he/she believes the international union may attempt to control the local membership.
    c. Make speeches to massed assemblies of employees on company time within a 24 hour period of time before the election.
    d. Speak to employees one-on-one in the office of the management official and urge them to vote against the union.

29. The first step in establishing an HRIS is to:

    a. develop the database.
    b. determine the information needs.
    c. establish a security and control system.
    d. select between PC and mainframe applications.

30. Underutilization is defined as having fewer minorities or women in a job classification than would be expected based on:

a. the area population.
b. their availability in the reasonable recruitment area.
c. their overall representation in the facility workforce.
d. the availability of required skills in the regional labor market.

31. Which of the following would be a recommended compensation practice for a start-up business that wishes to create an innovative, entrepreneurial culture?

a. Offer incentive bonuses and stock ownership plans.
b. Establish high starting pay rates to attract the most talented employees.
c. Offer a benefits program that exceeds competitors.
d. Establish step or longevity-based pay increases.

32. In a matrix organizational structure:

a. employees have three or more supervisors.
b. two organizational structures exist at the same time.
c. productivity is enhanced because of strict functional accountability.
d. line authority is strengthened.

33. Which of the following generally represents the greatest cost factor for training provided to employees by their organization?

a. Space materials expenses.
b. Program developer salary cost.
c. Trainee hours lost from production.
d. Consulting fees and equipment costs.

34. A supervisor who has an employee with a suspected alcohol problem impacting performance should:

   a. confront the employee immediately about the alcohol problem.
   b. diagnose the employee's problem before trying to counsel him/her.
   c. document the situation before discussing the decreased performance with the employee.
   d. never expect the employee to return to his/her previous performance level.

35. Which of the following statements best describes diversity programs?

   a. Lawful reverse discrimination.
   b. Valuing differences.
   c. Assimilating differences.
   d. Required for government contractors.

36. In order for a position to qualify under the executive exemption to the Fair Labor Standards Act, the position must:

   a. be considered an officer of the organization.
   b. have a bachelor's degree or higher.
   c. direct the work of at least two other full-time employees.
   d. spend less than 30% of the time on nonexempt duties.

37. What kind of arbitrator is selected by the parties to serve on a single grievance case?

   a. An ad hoc arbitrator.
   b. An interest arbitrator.
   c. A permanent umpire.
   d. A tri-partite arbitrator.

38. If a group is highly cohesive, the individuals in the group are more likely to:

    a. play devil's advocate with each other.
    b. value group norms and goals.
    c. exhibit dysfunctional competition with group members.
    d. desire a strong automatic leadership style.

39. Contributory pension plans:

    a. require contributions by the employee who will benefit from the income upon retirement.
    b. are funded solely by employer contributions.
    c. must be funded by contributions by the employer from current income.
    d. prohibit employees from participating in another retirement plan simultaneously.

40. For virtual jobs performed by individuals shifting from project-to-project or working on cross-functional teams that change frequently, a job analysis must focus on the:

    a. competencies required and how they are assessed and maintained.
    b. knowledge, skills and abilities needed to perform the jobs.
    c. tasks, duties and responsibilities of the virtual employees.
    d. essential job functions needed for the changing jobs.

41. Adults learn BEST when the material to be taught is:

    a. standardized.
    b. integrated with their experience.
    c. presented in a classroom lecture format.
    d. geared to the level that is slightly more difficult than they can easily handle.

42. Which of the following is an independent contractor?

   a. A temporary programmer who works part-time in the data processing department for $9 an hour.
   b. An auditor who performs a two-week audit of the company's financial records each year.
   c. A salesperson who has an office in his or her home and reports to a national sales manager.
   d. An executive who has an employment contract with a company regarding change of control.

43. Major changes to supporting cultures in mature organizations should occur:

   a. regularly once every 5 years to keep pace with competitors.
   b. with each new yearly business cycle.
   c. infrequently, no more than once every 7-10 years.
   d. rarely, only once or twice during the organization's life cycle in order to minimize the negative effects of change.

44. A data entry person earned $8.00 per hour plus a weekly attendance incentive of $20.00. If the employee works 42 hours in a work week, how much total compensation should be paid?

   a. $356.00.
   b. $364.00.
   c. $365.50.
   d. $372.00.

45. How could the heavy use of employee referrals for job vacancies violate nondiscrimination laws?

   a. By minority employees refusing to refer job applicants.
   b. Where it results in an undesirable status quo of an under represented workforce.
   c. Where minority employees constitute the majority of employees in the workforce.
   d. Where an Affirmative Action plan is not required to correct an imbalance.

46. If a candidate is recruited and hired through two professional employment agency contacts and both agencies claim the fee for the referral, what is the best approach to settling the claims?

    a. Pay the fee at 50 percent of each agency since both made the referral.
    b. Pay the full fee to each agency, since both agencies referred the candidate.
    c. Recommend the two agencies negotiate the fee, since only one fee is to be paid.
    d. Examine the referral documents as to dates referred and pay the fee to the agency whose referral was received first.

47. If the union asks the employer for use of company vehicles when not needed for work to transport their members to a union picnic, what is the proper response?

    a. Decline the request.
    b. Offer the use at a standard market price.
    c. Offer the use for a charge of gas and oil.
    d. Offer the use for a nominal fee.

48. Which action could improve the effectiveness of assessment centers in selecting employees from within the firm for higher-level positions?

    a. Self-nomination.
    b. Greater emphasis on interpersonal skills.
    c. Greater use of staff T&D people.
    d. Minimal participation by line managers.

49. What is a draw, as used for sales representatives?

    a. Money that is to be used to pay for traveling expenses.
    b. Money that is paid on a regular basis in addition to commissions.
    c. Money that is paid on a regular basis but that must be earned from commissions or paid back.
    d. Money that is paid on a regular basis to be applied against commissions but not paid back if unearned.

50. The HR control process is normally thought of as containing the following steps: I.) comparing actual with expected performance; II.) observing and measuring performance; III.) setting expectations or standards; and IV.) taking corrective action. What is the proper sequence of these steps?

   a. I, II, III, IV.
   b. II, I, IV, III.
   c. IV, II, III, I.
   d. III, II, I, IV.

51. If an HR practitioner developed an economic or statistical model to identify costs and benefits associated with an HR program, this would be called a(n):

   a. HR audit.
   b. human resource accounting.
   c. break-even analysis.
   d. utility analysis.

52. Simulation and gaming training is most often directed toward improvements in:

   a. decision-making.
   b. human relation problem solving.
   c. diversity initiatives.
   d. culture.

53. The most accepted method of calculating turnover rate is to compute for a given period the:

   a. ratio of new hires to total workforce.
   b. ratio of separations to total workforce.
   c. ratio of people who quit to new hires.
   d. number of separations in a particular department or unit.

54. For many years, employees at a certain company took two daily 10-minute coffee breaks. After being organized, the company received a request for two 15-minute coffee breaks. The company should:

   a. discontinue its practice.
   b. continue its practice and negotiate.
   c. discontinue its practice and negotiate.
   d. continue the practice but refuse to negotiate.

55. Which of the following is NOT included in a party-in-interest as defined by ERISA?

   a. Employee with less than one year of service.
   b. Owner of at least 50% of the property of the employer.
   c. Trustees, custodians and persons providing services to such a plan.
   d. Administrators, fiduciaries and trustees of an employee benefit plan.

56. Which of the following concerning benefits is of strategic importance and should be addressed by an organization?

   a. The cost of FMLA leave and other required leave.
   b. The mix between indirect and direct compensation.
   c. The tax consequences for employees of the benefits.
   d. The provision of government mandated benefits.

57. An organization that desires to use a job analysis method that allows for a quick response rate and gathering of data on a large number of jobs, should use which method of job analysis?

   a. Observation.
   b. Interview.
   c. Questionnaire.
   d. Functional Job Analysis.

58. An HR audit is a(n):

    a. attempt to quantify the value of its human resources to the organization.
    b. aggregate skills inventory of the organization's human resources.
    c. formal research effort to evaluate the current state of human resource management within the organization.
    d. part of a human resource accounting system.

59. What is one of the most frequently encountered practical challenges associated with the use of case studies?

    a. There are no final or absolute solutions in case studies.
    b. They are relatively unavailable in package form in the training marketplace.
    c. The instructor must select a case with which the training group can identify.
    d. Trainees are overzealous in wanting to apply their case solutions to real life.

60. Good faith bargaining requires that both labor and management:

    a. reach agreement on the mandatory items under negotiation.
    b. meet and discuss those mandatory items brought up by the other side.
    c. fairly represent themselves by not making inflammatory statements about the other side.
    d. reach agreement on all mandatory and permissive items brought up by the other side.

61. Which of the following methods of organizational development has been criticized for the emotional stress it creates for some participants?

    a. Team building.
    b. Transactional analysis.
    c. Sensitivity training.
    d. Survey feedback.

62. For which of the following types of employees are maturity curves most used as a basis of compensation?

    a. Executives.
    b. Management trainees.
    c. Professional personnel.
    d. Long service nonexempt employees.

63. To measure total organizational hiring costs, which of the following is most appropriate to consider?

    a. Only budgeted expenditures.
    b. Direct out-of-pocket expenditures.
    c. Both indirect and direct costs.
    d. Cost data supplied by the Department of Labor.

64. Employers under the OSHA Bloodborne Pathogens standard must:

    a. provide free hepatitis B vaccinations to all employees.
    b. establish a written exposure control plan.
    c. communicate an employee's bloodborne infection status to co-workers upon request.
    d. conduct regular blood tests on all employees.

65. The Worker Adjustment and Retraining Notification Act (WARN) of 1988 requires:

    a. severance pay to workers who lose their jobs permanently.
    b. sixty days notice if a mass layoff or facility closing is to occur.
    c. full disclosure regarding reasons for plant closing.
    d. a re-education allowance to workers over age 60.

66. Which of the following constitutes an intrinsic reward?

    a. Pay.
    b. Working conditions.
    c. The job itself.
    d. Complimentary supervision.

67. In order to reduce information overload, orientation programs should:

a. be modularized and spread out over a period of time.
b. be conducted only after an employee has served on the job for a specified period of time.
c. include a detailed employee reference manual for later use.
d. provide continuous feedback to participants.

68. The primary test to determine the reasonableness of a work rule is whether or not the:

a. union has requested a change in the rule or its elimination.
b. rule furthers a strict disciplinary approach to managing the workforce.
c. employees agree that the rule is necessary if the plant is to operate efficiently.
d. rule is reasonably related to a legitimate business reason.

69. One advantage of having an executive search firm on retainer is that:

a. search firms are ethically bound not to approach employees of client companies in their search efforts for another client.
b. it establishes an ongoing professional relationship that enables positions to be filled more efficiently.
c. search firms give their clients first refusal of an outstanding candidate.
d. in the long run, they are less expensive.

70. During negotiations the union and company were discussing wage increases for production operators. The company claimed that granting a wage increase would give the operators more money than the supervisors were making. The union requested the salary schedules for supervisors. What is the company required to do?

a. Refuse the request.
b. Provide the supervisors' salary schedule to the union.
c. Refuse the request, but give the information to a mediator.
d. Ignore the request.

71. Which of the following is not used as a method to segment a relevant labor market?

    a. Geographic.
    b. Type of skill.
    c. Income level.
    d. Industry.

72. In training supervisors for handling discipline and discharge incidents, which of the following is the most appropriate training method?

    a. On-the-job.
    b. Case study.
    c. Programmed instruction.
    d. Role-play.

73. What is the most important requirement for a qualified benefit plan in order to be eligible for favorable tax status?

    a. The plan must integrate with Social Security.
    b. The plan must not discriminate in favor of highly compensated executives.
    c. The plan must shift income to post-working retirement years.
    d. The plan must provide some type of retirement annuity.

74. A weighted application form is most appropriate for which type of position?

    a. Top level executive positions.
    b. Multiple incumbent positions.
    c. Positions that have underutilization of minorities.
    d. Unskilled positions.

75. An employee reports to work one morning with a weird hairstyle in order to impress the supervisor. The supervisor ignores this new hairstyle with the expectation that it will not be repeated. What type of behavior modification strategy was employed?

   a. Extinction.
   b. Punishment.
   c. Negative reinforcement.
   d. Positive reinforcement.

76. If many people perform a similar set of tasks, what would be the preferred method of collecting information for assessing training needs?

   a. Job inventory questionnaire.
   b. Employee opinion.
   c. Observation and interview.
   d. Performance appraisal data.

77. A manager summons a unionized employee to the manager's office to be interviewed about a work rule violation. The employee demands a union representative be present. Which of the following responses should the manager give?

   a. The meeting will be conducted without the union representative present, because it is management's right to discipline.
   b. No grievance has been filed so there is no entitlement to union representation.
   c. A union representative is only permitted if the contract provides for union representation at discipline meetings.
   d. A union representative may be present for investigative meetings that lead to discipline if requested by the employee.

78. According to workers' compensation law, payment of compensation is made to an employee for any injury:

   a. without regard to who is at fault.
   b. only when it is due to the employer's negligence.
   c. except one due to the employee's carelessness.
   d. except for one due to the negligence of a co-worker.

79. As a holiday absence control practice, employers commonly:

   a. require employees to work the day before and after a holiday to be eligible for holiday pay.
   b. provide employees flexibility as to holidays they want off.
   c. pay time and one-half to hourly employees who work the holiday in lieu of holiday pay.
   d. require employees to use vacation days if they don't work on a holiday.

80. If an HR manager notices the posting of a number of pin-ups—foldouts of scantily clothed females—out on the shop floor, the HR manager should have the posters removed based upon which theory of sexual harassment?

   a. Employment consequence.
   b. Employment conditions.
   c. Vicarious liability.
   d. Hostile environment.

81. Compensatory time off for non-exempt employees can be given in the private sector if:

   a. the hourly wage is at least one and one-half times the minimum wage.
   b. it is equivalent to the number of hours worked overtime within the same workweek.
   c. it is used within the next three months by the employee.
   d. it is given at the rate of one and one-half times hours worked over a 40-hour week.

82. It is not discriminatory during pre-employment inquiries to ask about an applicant's record on:

   a. workers' compensation.
   b. driving.
   c. arrests.
   d. favoring unions.

83. A salary survey shows the following data:

Organization	Number Incumbents	Average Salary
A	15	$ 700
B	10	700
C	25	700
D	50	800

How does the weighted average salary compare to the unweighted average salary?

a. It is $50 lower.
b. It is $25 lower.
c. It is $25 higher.
d. It is $50 higher.

84. In a firm's training and development program, the trainee must believe that improved skills will lead to desired outcomes and that his or her effort in the training program will result in improved skills. These assumptions are related to which theory of motivation?

a. Expectancy theory.
b. Reinforcement theory.
c. Motivation-hygiene theory.
d. Equity theory.

85. Leadership research has identified two major leader behaviors; one of which focuses on people and interpersonal relationships. What is the focus of the other?

a. Power and authority.
b. Task accomplishment.
c. Organizational culture.
d. Profitability and financial accountability.

86. When significant aspects of performance are not measured by the appraisal form, this is called:

a. criterion contamination.
b. criterion deficiency.
c. rater bias error.
d. contrast error.

87. Which of the following constitutes a major function of the Federal Mediation and Conciliation Service?

    a. Representing employees under the National Labor Relations Act.
    b. Advising companies and unions regarding the handling of grievances.
    c. Helping companies and unions to reach agreement during contract negotiations.
    d. Representing employees who feel they have been discriminated against based on their civil rights.

88. An applicant who was previously fired for misconduct by another employer does not list that employment experience on the application form and is subsequently hired. One month later, this omission is discovered. How should this situation be handled?

    a. The incident should be overlooked and considered a casual omission.
    b. The employee should receive a written disciplinary letter over the incident.
    c. The employee should be fired for falsification of the application.
    d. The previous employer should be contacted to determine the cause of the prior dismissal.

89. What is the most important factor contributing to success of a TQM program in an organization?

    a. Organizational culture supports the TQM program.
    b. Union acceptance of the TQM program.
    c. Statistical aptitude of supervisors in quality control.
    d. Individual rather than group awards for performance.

90. ERISA imposes which of the following on compensation systems:

    a. funding requirements.
    b. competitive compensation rates.
    c. arbitration procedures.
    d. mandatory pension plans.

91. Which of the following subject areas receive greatest emphasis in organizational sales training programs aimed at experienced and inexperienced salespersons?

    a. Product knowledge.
    b. Marketing orientation.
    c. Selling techniques.
    d. Company orientation.

92. If a supervisor gives an employee a very high rating on "quality of work" and allows that rating to influence the rating on "quantity of work," the supervisor is guilty of:

    a. leniency error.
    b. central tendency error.
    c. rater bias error.
    d. halo/horned error.

93. In translating the results of a salary survey into actual wage rates, what statistical technique would be most appropriate to use?

    a. Least-squares method.
    b. Dispersion method.
    c. Correlation method.
    d. Expected variance method.

94. An employment interviewer says to a job applicant "...that experience sounds interesting...," after which he or she pauses, waiting for the applicant to elaborate further. What type of interview technique is being used?

    a. Behavioral.
    b. Stress Interview technique.
    c. Non-directive interviewing technique.
    d. Patterned interview.

95. Which of the following factors is not related to pay compression?

   a. Higher starting salaries dictated by increased market pressures.
   b. Unionized hourly pay increases that overtake supervisory and non-union hourly rates.
   c. Merit increases that reward existing employees for higher productivity.
   d. Recruitment of new college graduates at pay levels above those current job holders.

96. In performance appraisal systems, central tendency is the most common error found in using:

   a. essays.
   b. ranking.
   c. critical incidents.
   d. graphic rating scales.

97. Which of the following BEST describes the relationship between human resource planning and strategic organizational planning?

   a. Human resource planning is the essential component of strategic organizational planning.
   b. They are separate and distinct activities.
   c. Human resource planning must be completed before strategic organizational planning begins.
   d. Both types of planning are equivalent components of overall organizational planning.

98. Which of the following approaches will most effectively minimize employee-relations difficulties?

   a. Install a suggestion system.
   b. Increase the amount of supervision provided employees.
   c. Maintain an open line of direct and factual communication with employees.
   d. Implement a quality control program.

99. After implementing a new job evaluation plan, it is best to deal with red circle rates by:

   a. reducing their salary to the new maximum for their respective job grade.
   b. allowing their base rate to increase as all others do in the same job grade.
   c. reducing the salary to the minimum of the range and providing the employee the amount of the decrease in the form of a bonus.
   d. freezing their salary until job grade maximum increases to catch up with the red circle rate.

100. The use of an aptitude test in a selection program best predicts:

   a. skill level.
   b. job knowledge.
   c. manual dexterity.
   d. training performance.

101. Which of the following training methods would be most appropriate to use to help a new manager develop planning and conceptual skills?

   a. Sensitivity training.
   b. Human relations training.
   c. Simulation training.
   d. Role-play training.

102. Why are skill tests more accurate in predicting failures than successes?

   a. They assess "can do" rather than "will do".
   b. The scores are more reliable in lower ranges than higher ranges.
   c. If applicants fail a test there is no certainty they will be unsuccessful on the job.
   d. They are designed to eliminate potential failures rather than identify potential successes.

103. The total span of possible work hours in a flex-time environment is referred to as:

    a. core time.
    b. bandwidth time.
    c. compressed work time.
    d. contingent time.

104. Multisource assessments (360 degrees appraisals) are most relevant and useful for:

    a. retention decisions.
    b. developmental purposes.
    c. merit pay decisions.
    d. candidates for international assignments.

105. If a labor relations manager discovers that an above-average union employee who has been employed at the plant for 9 years falsified an employment application by stating that he/she lost his/her previous job from layoff when, in fact, he or she was discharged, what should the manager do?

    a. Suspend the employee for 30 days.
    b. Schedule a grievance hearing as soon as possible.
    c. Discharge the employee for falsification of the application.
    d. Make the employee aware of the discovery but take no formal disciplinary action.

106. What is the most prevalent problem associated with the use of employees attitude surveys?

    a. Surveys are administered in-house.
    b. Employees are informed of survey results.
    c. Survey results are not responded to by management.
    d. Surveys are administered prior to management perceiving a problem.

107. A selection test for fire fighters that requires all applicants to pull a 90 pound hose up three flights of stairs within a four minute period would suggest which type of validity?

   a. Predictive.
   b. Concurrent.
   c. Content.
   d. Construct.

108. A primary employer advantage of implementing a skill-based pay system is:

   a. increased compensation costs.
   b. increased employee productivity.
   c. reduction of training and development expenses.
   d. ease of administration.

109. Greater flexibility for employees can be built into a vacation leave program by:

   a. providing more vacation time.
   b. reducing the advance notice period.
   c. allowing a carry-over of unused leave.
   d. having supervisors assign leave time.

110. A safety manager who wanted to know if financial incentives would reduce accidents randomly selected two departments and offered employees bonuses for reducing accidents. The incidence rates of these two departments were compared with other departments. This study illustrates what kind of experiment?

   a. Case study.
   b. Laboratory study.
   c. Field experiment.
   d. Simulation.

111. The most fundamental step to dealing with the issue of violence in the workplace is for an HR manager to establish:

    a. a discipline system to deal with potentially violent employees.
    b. a selection system that screens out potentially violent applicants
    c. a violence response team.
    d. training for supervisors in identifying potentially violent employees.

112. The concept of trainee involvement and immediate feedback are most prominent in which of the following training methods?

    a. Lecture.
    b. Correspondence courses.
    c. Programmed instruction.
    d. Audio visual techniques.

113. In an arbitration proceeding, it is agreed by all parties that the action complained about is a very slight departure from what is required in the labor contract. In such a case, the arbitrator is most likely to present the rule of:

    a. reason.
    b. parole evidence.
    c. de minimis.
    d. management by exception.

114. The most adequate defense an employer has in a defamation of character law suit arising from providing reference information is:

    a. the absence of malice.
    b. that the information given was the truth.
    c. that the employer had a qualified privilege to provide the information.
    d. that the employee signed a release.

115. In an organization adopting a pay-for-performance philosophy:

    a. a greater amount of employee pay is "at risk."
    b. cost of living increases are commonplace.
    c. length of service is used in calculating pay increases.
    d. external competitiveness dominates compensation decisions.

116. Which of the following activities of a firm would NOT be part of its social responsibility?

    a. Corporate giving.
    b. Environmental protection.
    c. Civil Rights Act compliance.
    d. Diversity training.

117. For a training program designed to enhance group problem solving skills, which type of seating management is most appropriate?

    a. Classroom style.
    b. Chevron style.
    c. Circle style.
    d. Theater style.

118. The least serious OSHA violation is:

    a. other-than-serious.
    b. de minimis.
    c. serious.
    d. willful and repeated.

119. Which of the following cannot be included in a salesperson's deductions for travel expenses for federal income tax purposes?

    a. Meal expenses.
    b. Lodging expenses.
    c. Entertainment expenses.
    d. Home-to-work commuting allowances.

120. Under the Drug Free Workplace Act (1988), an employer with government contracts worth more than $25,000 must do all of the following EXCEPT:

    a. terminate employees for off-time job drug usage.
    b. inform employees of drug-free requirements.
    c. outline actions to be taken.
    d. establish awareness programs and supervisory training.

121. In developing an international HR program, which factor is most critical to the success of an expatriate assignment in a foreign country?

   a. Equalizing negative tax consequences.
   b. Adaptation of spouse and family to a foreign country.
   c. Providing for security of expatriate and family.
   d. Readjustment training upon repatriation.

122. When a grievance goes to final and binding arbitration, arbitrators base their decisions on:

   a. their interpretation of the language of the labor agreement.
   b. the intent of the parties when the labor agreement was negotiated
   c. past arbitration dealing with the same issue in different organizations.
   d. the position of the National Labor Relations Board on the issue.

123. Tests would likely be used for evaluating the results of training programs when which criterion is utilized?

   a. Reaction.
   b. Learning.
   c. Behavior.
   d. Results.

124. A medical examination as part of the selection process should be:

   a. conducted prior to making the selection decision.
   b. scheduled after an employment offer has been extended.
   c. eliminated as a result of the Americans With Disabilities Act.
   d. conducted on a random basis.

125. Which of the following presents the least ethical dilemma for an HR manager to address?

   a Specifically excluding salaries of low paying organizations from a survey of HR positions.
   b. Referring a qualified personal friend's resume for an open position in another department.
   c. Informing employees of the reasons for the dismissal of a co-worker.
   d. Discussing an injured employee's medical condition with co-workers.

END OF PRACTICE EXAM

QUICK SCORING KEY

Number	Answer	Topic Area	Number	Answer	Topic Area
1.	B	02-03	38.	B	05-02
2.	A	01-06	39.	A	04-07
3.	B	03-04	40.	A	02-04
4.	B	05-09	41.	B	03-02
5.	B	04-11	42.	B	05-01
6.	A	02-08	43.	C	01-01
7.	D	06-09	44.	C	04-01
8.	D	05-02	45.	B	02-06
9.	B	03-04	46.	D	02-06
10.	B	02-09	47.	A	05-01
11.	A	05-09	48.	A	02-08
12.	C	01-02	49.	C	04-10
13.	A	03-01	50.	D	01-06
14.	D	04-06	51.	D	01-06
15.	A	04-02	52.	A	03-03
16.	C	02-08	53.	B	02-16
17.	D	05-01	54.	B	05-10
18.	D	01-02	55.	A	04-01
19.	B	05-01	56.	B	04-06
20.	A	04-02	57.	C	02-02
21.	C	02-08	58.	C	01-06
22.	A	03-06	59.	C	03-03
23.	A	02-08	60.	B	05-10
24.	C	05-09	61.	C	01-07
25.	A	04-08	62.	C	04-02
26.	A	03-06	63.	C	02-14
27.	A	04-01	64.	B	06-01
28.	B	05-09	65.	B	05-01
29.	B	01-01	66.	C	02-02
30.	B	02-17	67.	A	02-13
31.	A	04-06	68.	D	05-04
32.	B	01-06	69.	B	02-06
33.	C	03-03	70.	B	05-10
34.	C	06-10	71.	C	04-03
35.	B	03-14	72.	D	03-03
36.	C	04-01	73.	B	04-01
37.	A	05-07	74.	B	02-09

Number	Answer	Topic Area
75.	A	05-02
76.	A	03-01
77.	D	05-08
78.	A	06-08
79.	A	04-08
80.	D	05-01
81.	B	04-01
82.	B	02-03
83.	C	04-03
84.	A	03-02
85.	B	01-09
86.	B	03-13
87.	C	05-10
88.	C	02-09
89.	A	01-06
90.	A	04-01
91.	A	03-04
92.	D	03-13
93.	A	04-02
94.	C	02-09
95.	C	04-02
96.	D	03-11
97.	A	01-03
98.	C	05-02
99.	D	04-02
100.	D	02-08
101.	C	03-03
102.	A	02-08
103.	B	05-02
104.	B	03-12
105.	D	05-07
106.	C	05-03
107.	C	02-04
108.	B	04-02
109.	C	04-08
110.	C	06-07
111.	B	06-11

Number	Answer	Topic Area
112.	C	03-03
113.	C	05-10
114.	B	02-09
115.	A	04-02
116.	C	01-07
117.	C	03-03
118.	B	06-01
119.	D	04-01
120.	A	05-04
121.	B	02-12
122.	A	05-08
123.	B	03-02
124.	B	02-10
125.	B	01-09

Functional Area:

01 Strategic Management

02 Workforce Planning and Employment

03 Human Resource Development

04 Compensation and Benefits

05 Employee and Labor Relations

06 Occupational Health, Safety and Security

ANSWERS AND RATIONALES FOR PRACTICE QUESTIONS

1.   **Answer:**   **b. Locker room attendant.**

A Bona Fide Occupational Qualification (BFOQ) is a limited exception to the anti-bias rules under the Civil Rights Act, the Age Discrimination in Employment Act and the Americans with Disabilities Act. A BFOQ may be established on the basis of religion, sex, or national origin or absence of disability if the requirement is necessary to the normal operations of a business. This is a strict burden of proof that falls to the employer. It is not available with respect to race or color. The locker room attendant requires monitoring of locker rooms designated for one sex. Based upon community standards, a specific sex could probably be specified and supported.

CODE: 02-03

2.   **Answer:**   **a. Industrial Relations Director.**

An Industrial Relations Director is responsible for only labor relations and safety functions. The other positions are responsible for all major HR functions.

CODE: 01-06

3.   **Answer:**   **b. Training department's overhead.**

The training department's overhead is an indirect cost spread out over all training programs. All other options are direct costs associated with a single training program.

CODE: 03-04

4. **Answer:** b. **The union seeking certification must represent only guards.**

Due to divided loyalties and a conflict of interest, the NLRB has determined that plant guards must be in a separate union from other plant employees. During a strike situation, guards are responsible for protecting company property. Separating the guards into a different bargaining unit helps alleviate this problem.

CODE: 05-09

5. **Answer:** b. **The principal residence is in the U.S.**

The Internal Revenue Service allows home travel expenses to be deducted from taxes but only if the travel was to the expatriate's principal residence within the United States. Other locations are not tax deductible.

CODE: 04-11

6. **Answer:** a. **Past performance.**

Industrial psychologists have an axiom that the best indicator or prediction of future performance is past performance. The more recent the past performance, the stronger the predictive value. The more long term the past performance, the stronger the predictive value.

CODE: 02-08

7. **Answer:** d. **Treatment outcome.**

Most employee assistance programs provide periodic reports to employers outlining program activity. To protect employee confidentiality, information is compiled in such a way to guarantee anonymity. Treatment outcome is almost never reported back to the employer. The other information-- initial diagnosis category, referral source and utilization--is typically found in EAP provider reports.

CODE: 06-09

8. **Answer:**   **d. Direct discussions between supervisors and employees.**

Personal communication between employees and supervisors is the most effective upward communication format. Research shows that competent first-line supervisors are critical for management to feel the pulse of the organization. While the other forms of upward communication may be valuable, they are less effective than personal communication between supervisors and employees.

CODE: 05-02

9. **Answer:**   **b. Human relations.**

All of the options except human relations can be objectively measured and quantified. Soft skills, such as human relations, can be observed but represent a challenge in terms of measurement.

CODE: 03-04

10. **Answer:**   **b. Do you have a job-related disability?**

Under the Americans with Disabilities Act (ADA), pre-employment inquiries about a disability are unlawful. The ADA requires a focus on essential job functions and whether the person can perform those functions with or without reasonable accommodations.

CODE: 02-09

11. **Answer:**   **a. Win a majority of the votes cast in an election.**

Much like political elections in the U.S., the NLRB requires a union to win a majority of the votes during a representation election in order to certify the union. It is important, then, that all eligible employees participate in the voting so a small minority does not determine the fate of many.

CODE: 05-09

12. **Answer:**   **c.**   **Labor market.**

All of the options are areas searched in an environmental scan. The three factors listed are all factors of the relevant labor market.

CODE: 01-02

13. **Answer:**   **a.**   **Conducting a job/task analysis.**

A basic way to insure content validity of training programs is to conduct a job/task analysis. The other options are less related to content validity.

CODE: 03-01

14. **Answer:**   **d.**   **They overestimate the pay of their peers and underestimate that of their supervisors.**

Research (Lawler, 1972; Milkovich and Anderson, 1972) indicates that employees overestimate the pay of their peers and underestimate the pay of supervisors. The greater the overestimation, the greater the level of dissatisfaction with pay. As a result of this research, more organizations are moving away from pay secrecy to more open pay systems.

CODE: 04-06

15. **Answer:**   **a.**   **6.25%**

Count up the remaining months of the increase for January (12), March (10), July (6), and November (2) (equals 30 months at $100 month). Divide $3,000 by the total starting payroll costs $48,000. The increase is 6.25%.

CODE: 04-02

16. **Answer: c.   Reference checking.**

Negligent hiring is a tort law theory which holds that if an employer who hired an employee knew (or should have known) about a prior behavior of the employee that could cause harm to a third party, then the employer is liable if the employee subsequently causes harm to someone. Negligent hiring makes it extremely important for employers to thoroughly check background references on all employees who are in a position of trust or where their actions could harm others.

CODE: 02-08

17. **Answer: d.   100.**

The EEOC requires all employers with 100 or more employees to annually file an EEO-I report. The report numbers vary by type of organization.

EEO-1	Private Business
EEO-2	Joint Apprenticeship Committees
EEO-3	Unilateral Apprenticeship Programs
EEO-4	State and Local Governments
EEO-5	Public Elementary and Secondary Schools
EEO-6	Colleges and Universities

CODE: 05-01

18. **Answer: d.   Determining the relationship between personnel demand and the firm's output.**

The demand for human resources is often directly related to the expected demand for the firm's products and/or services. In addition, the organization's objectives and productivity are important determinants.

CODE: 01-02

19. Answer: b.   Ensure the selection of trainees is well docu-
                     mented and does not result in adverse impact.

Training is a condition of employment subject to EEO laws. As
such, participation opportunities come under the Uniform
Guidelines for Employee Selection Procedures (especially when
training opens up promotional opportunities). Adverse impact calculations should be made on selection of trainees using the 4/5's rule.

CODE: 05-01

20. Answer: a.   The company does not do much advertising.

Sales compensation is a function of identifying customers, persuad-
ing customers, and servicing customers. The more customer identification, often known as prospecting that is involved, the greater the
incentive opportunity should be available. Organizations that do lit-
tle advertising require more prospecting.

CODE: 04-02

21. Answer: c.   Examining each item and determining to
                     what extent it helped to predict job success.

An employment application form is considered a selection device
under the Uniform Guidelines for Employee Selection Procedures.
As such, if its use results in adverse impact, it should be evaluated.
The best approach is to validate it to job performance.

CODE: 02-08

22. Answer: a.   It permits employers to predict which additional
                     skills are needed for the workforce of the future.

A skills inventory is a listing of the skills, knowledge, abilities and
special qualifications of all employees in an organization. Employers
can use skills inventories to determine long range recruiting, selection and training needs. It is a critical aspect of workforce planning.

CODE: 03-06

23. **Answer:** a. **Aptitude.**

Interest tests such as the Strong-Campbell Interest Blank and the Kuder Preference Record are helpful in making selection and training decisions. They are also quite useful for counseling purposes. Personality inventories such as the Minnesota Multiphasic Personality Inventory measure some aspects of total personality. Specific abilities tests are used to measure a learned skill or knowledge about a specific occupation.

CODE: 02-08

24. **Answer:** c. **Organizational opposition to unions.**

An organization can legally state opposition to the unionization of employees. A pay increase for remaining non-union is a promise that constitutes an unfair labor practice. Likewise, a plant closure is a threat and also an unfair labor practice if done only to avoid the union. Endorsement of a specific union is also an unfair labor practice that could be construed as setting up a "company union."

CODE: 05-09

25. **Answer:** a. **Allow employees to contribute pretax dollars to buy additional benefits.**

The primary benefit of a flexible benefit plan involves favorable tax treatment under the Internal Revenue Code. Employees are able to use pretax dollars to purchase additional benefits.

CODE: 04-08

26. **Answer:** a. **Fall within perceptual and comprehension spans of the learners.**

Targeting content and training methods to the intended audience is critical to the success of training programs. Although culture, instructor, capability, and post-training transference are important, failure to accommodate the learners' capabilities affects training success more.

CODE: 03-06

27. **Answer:** a. **2 years.**

The FLSA has a two-year statute of limitation for recovery of back pay. In cases of a willful or intentional violation, a three-year statute of limitation is available. Records should be kept for this three-year period unless state law requires a more stringent standard.

CODE: 04-01

28. **Answer:** b. **Inform the employees that he/she believes the international union may attempt to control local membership.**

Employers are free to educate employees as long as they do not spy, threaten, coerce or promise. Employers can make speeches to employees (captive audiences), but not within 24 hours of an election. Visiting the homes of employees and one-on-one discussions in management offices are clearly out of bounds.

CODE: 05-09

29. **Answer:** b. **Determine the information needs.**

An HRIS supports organizational decision making, therefore, the first step is to determine the specific information needs. The other options, while important, should follow the information needs analysis.

CODE: 01-01

30. **Answer:** b. **Their availability in the reasonable recruitment area.**

The Office of Federal Contract Compliance Programs defines underutilitzation in relation to "the government contractor's reasonable recruitment area." That area involves where the contractor recruits or could be expected to recruit.

CODE: 02-17

31. Answer: a. **Offer incentive bonuses and stock ownership plans.**

Incentive bonuses and stock plans both focus employee behavior on building the company. They allow employees to share in the success of the company. High fixed-cost compensation programs are not appropriate for start-up organizations.

CODE: 04-06

32. Answer: b. **Two organizational structures exist at the same time.**

With a matrix organizational structure, two organizational structures exist at the same time--a conventional functional organization and a project team organization. Employees join a project team but retain their positions in the conventional organization. Matrix structures are often prevalent in new product development.

CODE: 01-06

33. Answer: c. **Trainee hours lost from production.**

Time away from the job represents a significant cost of training programs for employees. Work goes undone, supervisors or coworkers fill in or overtime is incurred due to absences due to training. These expenses generally far exceed other training-related costs.

CODE: 03-03

34. Answer: c. **Document the situation before discussing the decreased performance with the employee.**

In general, supervisors are ill-equipped to handle alcohol-related problems in the workplace. They should not confront nor counsel someone suffering from alcoholism, but should address the situation as a performance problem and refer the employee to professional help.

CODE: 06-10

35. **Answer:** b. **Valuing differences.**

Diversity programs help employees understand, appreciate and value others who may be different than themselves. It represents a culture change away from ethnocentrism and exclusivity toward inclusiveness and community.

CODE: 03-14

36. **Answer:** c. **Direct the work of at least two other full-time employees.**

Under the FLSA, an executive must have as primary management duties; the supervision of two or more full-time employees, routinely exercise discretion, have authority to hire or fire, spend less than 20% of their time on nonexempt work, and be paid a salary of $155 per week or more.

CODE: 04-01

37. **Answer:** a. **An ad hoc arbitrator.**

An ad hoc arbitrator sits on a per case basis. An interest arbitrator is used not in grievance but in collective bargaining. A permanent umpire serves as an arbitrator for the life of the labor contract. A tri-partite arbitrator is really an arbitration panel of three persons that may be ad hoc or permanent in nature.

CODE: 05-07

38. **Answer:** b. **Value group norms and goals.**

Sometimes cohesive groups value group norms and goals in detrimental ways, such as the "group think" phenomena. However, a cohesive group is generally easier to lead to goal attainment.

CODE: 05-02

39. **Answer:**   a. **Require contributions by the employee who will benefit from the income upon retirement.**

Contributory pension plans require contributions by the employee who will benefit from the income upon retirement. Non-contributory pension plans do not require any contributions by employees. Non-contributory pension plans are popular because employees do not receive tax breaks on current earnings on contributions they make and tax laws create administrative burdens on plans that permit employee contributions.

CODE: 04-07

40. **Answer:**   a. **Competencies required and how they are assessed and maintained.**

Because of the changing nature of virtual jobs, the traditional emphasis on knowledge, skills and abilities and essential job functions is not flexible enough to meet the requirements of the virtual workplace where multi-faceted competencies determine success.

CODE: 02-04

41. **Answer:**   b. **Integrated with their experience.**

Adult learning differs from other forms of learning in that trainee experience can be integrated into the learning process to make the learning process more meaningful. Traditional learning models such as classroom lecture and programmed instruction do not allow the flexibility of experiential development.

CODE: 03-02

42. **Answer:** **b. An auditor who performs a two-week audit of the company's financial records each year.**

The Internal Revenue Service has established a 20-factor test in making an independent contractor determination. Primary factors include: does the individual own their own facilities or equipment? Is there an opportunity to make a profit or loss? Are the services available to others? How much supervision is exercised?

CODE: 05-01

43. **Answer:** **c. Infrequently, once every 7-10 years.**

Changes to organizational culture should not be undertaken often. Such changes should be thoroughly researched, planned and implemented over a period of years. This is especially true for more stable organizations with mature cultures. Usually, cultural changes in such organizations take a considerable amount of time.

CODE: 01-01

44. **Answer:** **c. $365.50.**

In calculating overtime, incentive/bonus money is figured in the base rate to determine the overtime rate (1.5 times base). Calculation is 40 hours x $8/hr = $320 for regular base rate. Overtime rate is $320 plus $20 = $340 ($8.50/hr) x 1.5 or $12.75/hr. Total compensation is $320 base rate plus $20 bonus plus $24.00 (2 hrs x $12.75) overtime for $365.50.

CODE: 04-01

45. **Answer:** **b. Where it results in an undesirable status quo of an under-represented workforce.**

Recruitment by "word of mouth" through current employees may create EEO problems. An under-represented workforce will usually refer applicants like the workforce itself. The effect of such recruitment is to perpetuate past discrimination.

CODE: 02-06

46. **Answer:** d. **Examine the referral documents as to dates referred and pay the fee to the agency whose referral was received first.**

Although the other options all seem plausible, the HR manager is faced with an issue of contract law. The rule of thumb is that the first to refer receives the fee. Most agency contracts contain language to that effect.

CODE: 02-06

47. **Answer:** a. **Decline the request.**

Under Section 8 of the National Labor Relations Act (Wagner Act), it is an unfair labor practice for an employer to dominate or interfere with the information or administration of any labor organization or to contribute financial or other support to it. The use of company vehicles would be viewed as supporting the union.

CODE: 05-01

48. **Answer:** a. **Self-nomination.**

While the cost of assessing every person at particular levels may be prohibitive, reliance on supervisors to nominate participants also presents difficulties. Employee attributes considered important at higher levels may not be valued by supervisors in lower levels of the firm.

CODE: 02-08

49. **Answer:** c. **Money that is paid on a regular basis, but that must be earned from commissions or paid back.**

A draw is an amount advanced and repaid from future commissions. A draw system allows salespersons to even out compensation between high and low sales periods. A risk to employers is that future commission may not be large enough to cover the draw.

CODE: 04-10

50. **Answer: d. III, II, I, IV.**

Much like setting the temperature on a thermostat, the HR control process involves setting expectations/standards, observing/measuring performance, comparing actual to expected performance, and taking corrective action if necessary.

CODE: 01-06

51. **Answer: d. Utility analysis.**

A utility analysis builds an economic or statistical model to identify the costs and benefits associated with specific HR programs or activities. Utility analysis is one of the basic ways to establish the worth of HR programs.

CODE: 01-06

52. **Answer: a. Decision-making.**

Simulation and gaming is used most often to improve decision-making. Simulation is a development that requires the trainee to analyze a situation and decide a best course of action based on the data given.

CODE: 03-03

53. **Answer: b. The ratio of separations to total workforce.**

The Department of Labor approved the following formula for calculating turnover:

$$\frac{\text{Number of Terminations} \times 100}{\text{Average Number of Employees}}$$

Turnover rates should be calculated for more fuller understanding. Rates can be calculated by facility, department, longevity, performance level, demographic group, etc. for a more detailed analysis of turnover pockets.

CODE: 02-16

54. **Answer: b. Continue its practice and negotiate.**

Coffee breaks are a mandatory subject for negotiation. However, the employer is under no obligation to change past practice until the item has been negotiated. Unions often attempt to change past practice outside of the bargaining environment. The employer's best strategy is to deal with the issue through the formalized structure of collective bargaining.

CODE: 05-10

55. **Answer: a. Employees with less than one year of service.**

Under ERISA, a party-in-interest includes all individuals who come under or have impact on a qualified plan. Owners, trustees, administrators, etc., are all considered a party-in-interest. Until an individual becomes a plan participant, they are not considered a party-in-interest.

CODE: 04-01

56. **Answer: b. The mix between indirect and direct compensation.**

Although all options are important to designing and administering employee benefit plans, only the mix between indirect compensation (benefits) and direct compensation (pay) can be controlled by the organization. The mix becomes an important element in a total compensation or rewards strategy.

CODE: 04-06

57. **Answer:**   **c.**   **Questionnaire.**

Questionnaires, as a means of gathering job-analysis data, provide the most efficient use of resources when data must be collected on many jobs. Questionnaires are self-administered, allowing them to be given to many participants at once. They may be open-ended to allow great flexibility or highly structured to fit compensation or validation needs. Observation is very time consuming, especially for long cycle jobs. Likewise, individual interviews require quite a bit of time. Functional job analysis, used by the federal government, is highly structured and requires extensive resources.

CODE: 02-02

58. **Answer:**   **c.**   **A formal research effort to evaluate the current state of human resource management within the organization.**

An HR audit is a systematic study of the HR functions performed–or not performed–in the organization and identifies strengths, weaknesses and corrective action.

CODE: 01-06

59. **Answer:**   **c.**   **The instructor must select a case with which the training group can identify.**

Case studies represent an excellent form of development as long as learning transfer back to the workplace takes place. A key factor in this transferability is the relevance of the case situation and trainee identification with the case.

CODE: 03-03

60. **Answer:** b. **Meet and discuss those mandatory items brought up by the other side**

Good-faith bargaining does not require either side to agree to anything. The only requirement is that they meet and discuss the mandatory issues raised by the other side. Good faith is measured by the totality of the conduct of the party.

CODE: 05-10

61. **Answer:** c. **Sensitivity training.**

Organizational development (OD) is designed to increase an organization's effectiveness through planned interventions using behavioral science knowledge. A number of techniques are used in OD, including sensitivity training. This method makes individuals aware of themselves and the impact they have on others. Sensitivity training features an unstructured group with no specific agenda. The interaction that takes place in these groups is apparently quite threatening to some people.

CODE: 01-07

62. **Answer:** c. **Professional personnel**

Maturity curves are a compensation plan that depicts the relationship between experience in a career field and pay level. They are most appropriate to professionals in science, engineering, architecture and related fields.

CODE: 04-02

63. **Answer:** c. **Both indirect and direct costs.**

In calculating total organizational hiring costs, all costs associated with turnover must be considered. Down time, lost productivity, and training time are a few of the cost factors that must be considered.

CODE: 02-14

64. **Answer:** b. **Establish a written exposure control plan.**

The OSHA Bloodborne Pathogens Standard requires employers subject to OSHA that have any employees with on-the-job exposure to blood or other bodily fluids to take the following steps:

1. Establish a written exposure control plan.
2. Observe universal precautions.
3. Identify and adopt engineering and work practice controls.
4. Provide personal protective equipment.
5. Develop housekeeping, waste management and laundry standards.
6. Make available free hepatitis B vaccinations to those employees with occupational exposure.
7. Establish post-exposure evaluation.
8. Communicate hazards to employees.
9. Maintain specific recordkeeping.

CODE: 06-01

65. **Answer:** b. **Sixty days notice if a mass layoff or facility closing is to occur.**

WARN was intended to provide affected workers, their union (if present), elected public officials and state employment services advance notice of impending mass layoffs and/or plant closings. Nothing in WARN requires severance pay, re-education or retraining allowances, or disclosure of the circumstances regarding the layoff or closing.

CODE: 05-01

66. **Answer:** c. **The job itself.**

Motivation can be categorized as extrinsic or intrinsic. Extrinsic motivation comes from the environment--pay, working conditions and supervision. Intrinsic motivation comes from within the employee--the work, challenge, and curiosity.

CODE: 02-02

67. **Answer:** a. **Be modularized and spread out over a period of time.**

Too much information given too fast creates information overload and reduces information retention. To minimize this problem, orientation activities should be divided into manageable units and spread out over time.

CODE: 02-13

68. **Answer:** d. **Rule is reasonably related to a legitimate business reason.**

Work rules cannot be arbitrary and capricious. They must relate to a legitimate business reason in order to be upheld.

CODE: 05-04

69. **Answer:** b. **It establishes an ongoing professional relationship that enables positions to be filled more efficiently.**

There are two types of executive search firms—contingency firms and retainer firms. Contingency firms charge a fee only after a candidate is hired by a client. Retained firms charge a set fee whether or not a contracted search has been successful. The ongoing relationship with a retained firm is a primary benefit over a contingency firm. Both types of firms are ethically bound not to approach current employees of clients.

CODE: 02-06

70. **Answer:** b. **Provide the supervisor's salary schedule to the union.**

Management has a duty to provide relevant information to a union for collective bargaining purposes. Determining what is relevant is often problematic. If a rationale for not granting a pay increase involves a pay compression problem with supervisors, the union is entitled to such information. If management did not use this rationale, it would be under no obligation to provide the supervisor's salary schedule.

CODE: 05-10

71. **Answer:**   c. **Income level.**

For compensation purposes, a relevant labor market is defined as the market from which an organization secures new employees from or to which they lose current employees. Income level is not a traditional labor market for survey purposes, whereas geographic, skill and industry represent relevant defined labor markets.

CODE: 04-03

72. **Answer:**   d. **Role-play.**

Role-play requires the trainee to assume a role in a mock situation and act out that role. It is behavioral-based and allows for feedback on the trainee's performance. Discipline and discharge training is ideally suited for role-playing.

CODE: 03-03

73. **Answer:**   b. **The plan must not discriminate in favor of highly compensated executives.**

The Internal Revenue Service has stated that for a benefit plan to qualify for tax favored status, it must be a definite written plan and arrangement that is communicated to the employees and established and maintained by an employer for the exclusive benefit of employees or beneficiaries. As such, the plan cannot discriminate in favor of certain highly-compensated employees.

CODE: 04-01

74. **Answer:**   b. **Multiple incumbent positions.**

Weighted applications are designed using job analysis and performance appraisal data. Certain responses are given weights or numerical scores based on performance data. Weighted applications are time-consuming and must be periodically validated the same as tests. Because of this, they are most appropriate for multiple incumbent positions.

CODE: 02-09

75. **Answer:** a. **Extinction.**

Extinction is ignoring behavior. Punishment includes sending the employee home until the hairstyle is changed. Negative reinforcement exists if the supervisor criticizes the hairstyle. Positive reinforcement involves the supervisor complimenting the employee on the hairstyle.

CODE: 05-02

76. **Answer:** a. **Job inventory questionnaire.**

Job inventory questionnaires can be administered to a large group of employees in a short amount of time to identify training needs. The other identified methods are more time consuming.

CODE: 03-01

77. **Answer:** d. **A union representative may be present for investigative meetings that lead to discipline if requested by the employee.**

Under the Weingarten decision (NLRB v. Weingarten, Inc. 420 U.S. 262, 1974), the U.S. Supreme Court ruled that union representation must be given to an employee when the employee requests representation and the he/she reasonably believes the investigation will result in disciplinary action.

CODE: 05-08

78. **Answer:** a. **Without regard to who is at fault.**

Workers' compensation is designed to provide no-fault coverage for work-related injuries and illnesses. The passage of workers' compensation statutes took away from employees the right to raise defenses of contributory negligence on the employee or co-worker's part and on the employer's part.

CODE: 06-08

79. **Answer:**   **a.   Require employees to work the day before and after a holiday to be eligible for holiday pay.**

The most common practice in traditional time off plans is the requirement that employees work the last scheduled day before and after a holiday in order to minimize the use of unscheduled absence such as sick leave. Many employers allow for scheduled pre-approved vacation days in conjunction with holidays to provide employees maximum use of available time off.

CODE: 04-08

80. **Answer:**   **d.   Hostile environment.**

Posting of pin-ups is an example of a hostile environment theory of sexual harassment. Under this theory, sexual harassment is not directed at one person but creates an environment that interferes with work performance. The use of sexually suggestive jokes can also be an example of the hostile environment theory. There are no employment conditions or consequences from the pin-up.

CODE: 05-01

81. **Answer:**   **b.   It is equivalent to the number of hours worked overtime within the same work week.**

Compensatory time off, or comp time, is time off given in lieu of payment of extra time worked. It is illegal in the private sector unless it is given at the rate of one and one-half times the base rate for hours worked in a 40 hour work week. It may not be carried over beyond the workweek. In the public sector, for police and fire employees and limited other employees, comp time may be "booked" up to a set number of hours.

CODE: 04-01

82. **Answer:**   **b. Driving.**

Asking about a driving record is legitimate if the future employee has to drive as part of his or her duties. Inquiries about workers' compensation may be illegal under the ADA. Inquiries about arrest records have a disproportionate impact on minority group members. Employers may not discriminate based upon union preference.

CODE: 02-03

83. **Answer:**   **c. It is $25 higher.**

The unweighted average salary is 700 + 700 + 700 + 800(2,900) divided by 4 = $725.

The weighted average salary is calculated as follows:
15 x 700	=	10,500
10 x 700	=	7,000
25 x 700	=	17,500
50 x 800	=	40,000
100		75,000 divided by 100 = $750

CODE: 04-03

84. **Answer:**   **a. Expectancy theory.**

Reinforcement theory holds that the consequences of behavior influence that behavior. To be most effective, reinforcement must be provided as soon after the desired behavior as possible. Herzberg's motivation - hygiene theory focuses on satisfiers or motivators (such as achievement and responsibility), and dissatisfiers, or hygiene factors which are important in preventing "demotivation" but do not positively motivate performance. Hygiene factors are company policy, working conditions, and pay. Equity theory suggests that individuals compare their rewards and the efforts required to reach them with the rewards and efforts of other relevant individuals.

CODE: 03-02

85. **Answer:** b. **Task accomplishment.**

This item comes from leadership research from Ohio State that identified two leader behaviors of consideration and initiating structure; University of Michigan researchers who identified production-centered and employee-centered leadership; and the Blake and Mouton Managerial Grid, which uses as its dimensions concerns for the task and concern for people.

CODE: 01-09

86. **Answer:** b. **Criterion deficiency.**

Criterion deficiency occurs when significant aspects of job performance are not captured by the appraisal instrument. Criterion contamination occurs when the appraisal instrument captures non-relevant factors to performance. Rater bias is the prejudice of the rater that influences ratings. Contrast error is rating one employee higher or lower, not because of objective performance but because of how they compare to another employee.

CODE: 03-13

87. **Answer:** c. **Helping companies and unions to reach agreement during contract negotiations.**

The Federal Mediation and Conciliation Service (FMCS) assists union/management negotiations when an impasse is reached. The FMCS attempts to keep the parties talking by finding common ground for further discussion. They try to forestall a strike or lockout.

CODE: 05-10

88. **Answer:** c. **The employee should be fired for falsification of the application.**

A commonly recognized principal-at-law is that fraudulent misrepresentation on an application is grounds for immediate dismissal. Additionally, falsification of official records is viewed as a serious violation of work rules. If an applicant intentionally lies or conceals information and was previously terminated by another employer for misconduct, it is safe to assume that additional problems will occur. The best indicator of future performance is past performance. The employee should be terminated.

CODE: 02-09

89. **Answer:** a. **Organizational culture supports the TQM program.**

Research shows the number one determinant of success in a total quality management program is support by all members of the organization. TQM is not a single technique, but a total philosophy for operating an organization. Although union acceptance of the TQM program and statistical aptitude of supervisors are factors that can affect success, they are far less important than organizational support.

CODE: 01-06

90. **Answer:** a. **Funding requirements.**

The Employee Retirement Security Act of 1974 (ERISA) was established to regulate various fringe compensation programs including medical, life and disability programs as well as pension programs. ERISA addresses employer reporting and disclosure, funding of benefits, fiduciary responsibilities and vesting rights.

CODE: 04-01

91. **Answer:**   a.   **Product knowledge.**

With differing experience levels among salesperson trainees, selling techniques would be a challenge for training. Most sales training programs with diverse participants focus on common content for trainees, in this case, product knowledge.

CODE: 03-04

92. **Answer:**   d.   **Halo/horned error.**

Allowing the rating of one area of performance to influence the rating of another area of performance is a criterion contamination problem frequently referred to as the halo/ horned effect. If the influence is positive, it is the halo effect. If the influence is negative, it is the horned effect. Leniency is rating all employees very high. Its opposite is strictness or rating all employees very low. Central tendency involves rating persons in a narrow band in the middle of a rating scale. Rater bias occurs when a rater's values or prejudices distorts the ratings.

CODE: 03-13

93. **Answer:**   a.   **Least squares method.**

The least squares method of regression analysis is a technique for fitting a line to data plotted on a graph to determine the degree of correlation (or significance) between two variables. In building a salary structure, the plotted line is referred to as the trend line and salary grades are based on it.

CODE: 04-02

94. **Answer:** **c.** **Non-directive interviewing technique.**

A non-directive interview uses general open-ended questions from which other probing questions can be asked. Non-directive interviews are less threatening to the interviewee and allow a broader discussion. A potential difficulty associated with non-directive interviews involves obtaining standardized information from interviewees.

CODE: 02-09

95. **Answer:** **c.** **Merit increases that reward existing employees for higher productivity.**

Pay compression exists when pay differentials between new hires and long-term employees are small or when pay differentials between supervisors and those supervised are small. Merit increases very seldom cause pay compression.

CODE: 04-02

96. **Answer:** **d.** **Graphic rating scales.**

Central tendency is a common problem associated with a performance appraisal that uses a graphic rating scale. The rater evaluates all employees as average or in the mid-range of the scale. In effect, the rater is not making any judgments.

CODE: 03-11

97. **Answer:** **a.** **Human resource planning is the essential component of strategic organizational planning.**

Human resource planning must flow from and complement strategic organizational planning. Strategic planning involves identifying organizational objectives and actions needed to achieve those objectives. Human resource planning involves analyzing the need for and availability (or unavailability) of human resources so that the organization can meet its objectives.

CODE: 01-03

98. **Answer:**   c. **Maintain an open line of direct and factual communication with employees.**

Research consistently shows that many employees are uninformed and misinformed in most organizations. The most effective employee relations initiative of the options provided is in communication. First-line supervisors are the key to keeping the lines of communication both open and factual.

CODE: 05-02

99. **Answer:**   d. **Freezing their salary until job grade maximum increases catch up with the red circle rate.**

A red circle rate is where the incumbent is paid above the rate range maximum for the job. Red circle rates come about either through the administration of a new job evaluation plan or when an employee may take a demotion. The standard practice for handling red circle rates is to freeze the incumbent's salary until such time as the range catches up to the rate.

CODE: 04-02

100. **Answer:**   d. **Training performance.**

An aptitude test measures accumulated learning from a number of sources. It measures one's capability as it relates to training performance. Other tests are more appropriate at predicting the other options.

CODE: 02-08

101. Answer: **c.**   **Simulation training.**

Simulation training uses a controlled training situation away from the work site. It provides realistic conditions in an environment where the consequences of errors can be minimized. Business cases and executive games are examples of simulations that are adaptable to planning and conceptual skills. Too often, simulation only brings to mind skill training such as drivers' education or flight training for pilots. The other options, sensitivity training, human relations training and role-playing are more appropriate techniques for personal interaction skills training.

CODE: 03-03

102. Answer: **a.**   **They assess "can do" rather than "will do".**

Performance is a function of skills and abilities multiplied by motivation. Skill tests measure whether the person has the skills necessary to perform the job. They measure aptitude, which in turn serves as a measure of capability. Skill tests do not predict motivation, and are better at predicting failures rather than successes.

CODE: 02-08

103. Answer: **b.**   **Bandwidth time.**

Bandwidth time refers to the total range of hours when employees can begin and end work. Core time refers to those hours when all employees must be at work. If an employee must work eight hours between 6 AM and 6 PM, the time between 6 AM and 6 PM is referred to as bandwidth time.

CODE: 05-02

104. Answer: b.   **Developmental purposes.**

Multisource assessments are also referred to as 360-degree feed-back, full-circle feedback and multirater assessment. First, critical competencies, behaviors or values are identified. Then managers are evaluated on these skill sets by having direct reports, internal and external customers, peers or co-workers, or superiors complete a confidential survey about the person's ability. The summarized data is shared with the manager for developmental purposes. Multisource assessments are popular in team environments.

CODE: 03-12

105. Answer: d.   **Make the employee aware of the discovery but take no formal disciplinary action.**

In this situation, the falsification occurred so long ago that it is highly unlikely an arbitration would uphold a grievance or termina-tion. A "stale" past record serves to set aside any disciplinary action especially given a good current performance record.

CODE: 05-07

106. Answer: c.   **Survey results are not responded to by management.**

Administering an attitude survey to employees implies that the results will be followed-up by management. If employees are to voluntarily participate in such surveys, they must believe that the feedback will result in change. Research indicates that the failure to share results and respond to problems significantly reduces partici-pation in subsequent surveys.

CODE: 05-03

107. **Answer:**   c.   **Content.**

Pulling a 90-pound hose up three flights of stairs represents an actual work sample for a fire fighter. Work samples are the most basic form of content validity. The test in this instance measures an actual content domain of the job.

CODE: 02-04

108. **Answer:**   b.   **Increased employee productivity.**

The primary employer advantage is increased productivity from a higher-skilled workforce. Additionally, skills-based pay system provides increased compensation to employees as they master and become certified in new skills. These systems are person-based, as opposed to job-based. They pay for skill mastery as opposed to responsibility. These plans provide both job enrichment and job security for employees. They allow for the opportunity to earn more pay. In practice, payroll costs are less because of increased workforce flexibility and decreased staffing.

CODE: 04-02

109. **Answer:**   c.   **Allowing a carry-over of unused leave.**

Accrual of vacation leave along with year-end carry-over allows employees to accumulate vacation leave for special occasions. If the amount of carryover is great, it can create a cash flow problem for employers when taken or paid-out upon termination.

CODE: 04-08

110. **Answer:**   c.   **Field experiment.**

A field experiment involves manipulating an independent variable (financial incentives) and measuring the effect on a dependent variable (incident rates). A case study involves analyzing an event and describing what happened. A laboratory study and a simulation both occur in a controlled environment as opposed to a natural work environment.

CODE: 06-07

111. Answer: b. **A selection system that screens out potentially violent applicants.**

"An ounce of prevention is worth a pound of cure," according to Benjamin Franklin. A selection system designed to assess risk factors and screen out those applicants is the best starting point. The other options, although important in a threat of violence program, should be preceded by an effective selection system. Such systems may include psychological testing, risk assessment interviewing, and reference checking.

CODE: 06-11

112. Answer: c. **Programmed instruction.**

Programmed instruction typically provides a small amount of information to the trainee and then poses a question. If the correct answer is given, the trainee is directed to the next "frame." If the incorrect response is given, the trainee is directed to restudy the information.

CODE: 03-03

113. Answer: c. **De minimis.**

Minor violations of a collective bargaining agreement are generally not accorded much weight by arbitrators. These "de minimis" violations, while technically wrong, do not generally result in substantial harm to either party. Only when a pattern of such "de minimis" violations is demonstrated will an arbitrator remedy in an award.

CODE: 05-10

114. Answer: **b.**   **That the information given was the truth.**

The ultimate or absolute defense in a defamation of character suit is the truth. For a plaintiff to prevail, he or she must show that the information provided was a lie. Although the other options to this item are defenses, the truth provides the most protection for the employer.

CODE: 02-09

115. Answer: **a.**   **A greater amount of employee pay is "at risk."**

Pay-for-performance systems are becoming very popular because of their perceived relationship to organizational performance. In a pay-for-performance system, no increases are given except when justified by objective measurable performance increases.

CODE: 04-02

116. Answer: **c.**   **Civil Rights Act compliance.**

Social responsibility is the idea that business has social obligations above and beyond making a profit. It goes beyond complying with the law—in this case, the Civil Rights Act. It is voluntary actions that result from the business helping itself to ultimately help others.

CODE: 01-07

117. Answer: **c.**   **Circle style.**

Circle and horseshoe seating arrangements are especially suited for highly interactive training such as group problem solving. Classroom, chevron and theater seating lend themselves to large group presentations with less trainer-participant interaction.

CODE: 03-03

118. **Answer:**   **b. De minimis.**

OSHA categorizes violations in the following manner--de minimis, other-than-serious, serious, willful and repeated, and imminent danger. A de minimis violation does not have a direct and immediate relationship to the employee's health and safety. An other-than-serious violation could have an impact on the employee's health and safety, but would not cause death or serious harm and the employer should know the condition. Willful and repeated violations occur when the employer has previously been cited by OSHA for the same condition.

CODE: 06-01

119. **Answer:**   **d. Home-to-work commuting allowances.**

The first three options are legitimate sales-related expenses that qualify under the Internal Revenue Codes as deductible expenses. Home-to-work travel is not a sales-related expense.

CODE: 04-01

120. **Answer:**   **a. Terminate employees for off-time job drug use.**

The Drug Free Workplace Act addresses only on-the-job drug use. Many employers refer employees with drug abuse problems to Employee Assistance Programs or other professional treatment sources.

CODE: 05-04

121. Answer: b. Adaptation of spouse and family to a
                      foreign country.

Although many factors affect the success of a foreign assignment, research consistently shows that the adjustment of spouse and family is the most critical factor. Employers too often do not give enough weight to this factor in developing their international HR programs. The focus tends to be on the expatriate and not his or her family.

CODE: 02-12

122. Answer: a. Their interpretation of the language of the
                      labor agreement.

Arbitrators are bound by the four-corners of the document, meaning they must interpret the specific language of the labor agreement. The labor agreement becomes controlling and the arbitration award is issued addressing the specific issue in question, under the specific clause of the labor agreement, in a specific organizational setting. As long as arbitrators act within the slope and bounds of their authority, their decisions can not be successfully appealed in the judicial system.

CODE: 05-08

123. Answer: b. Learning.

Training reaction to the value of training programs is probably the most frequent criterion used to evaluate training programs. In this approach, trainees are asked (often using questionnaires) whether the training is useful. Learning is what trainees can demonstrate that they know as a result of the training. Using tests, it can be determined if they have learned successfully. When behavior is the criterion, the focus is on whether the learning will be applied on the job. Behaviors are most likely to be measured through a performance appraisal system such as BARS. Trainees may believe the training to be useful (reaction), they may even use newly acquired techniques on the job (behavior). However, organizations should be interested in results.

CODE: 03-02

124. Answer: **b.   Scheduled after an employment offer has been extended.**

The Americans with Disabilities Act prohibits medical examinations before the extension of an employment offer. Results of a medical examination can then be used in making reasonable accommodations.

CODE: 02-10

125. Answer: **b.   Referring a qualified personal friend's resume for an open position in another department.**

Although all the options are potential ethical dilemmas for the HR manager, referring the resume of a qualified friend to an open position in another department is the least problematic. As long as the HR manager does not advocate for the selection of the friend, no ethics violation would occur. To deny the referral based on friendship would deny a qualified candidate equal opportunity. Skewing salary survey data for self-betterment is clearly an ethics violation. Likewise, breaches of confidentiality are ethics violations.

CODE: 01-09

SECTION V:

FREQUENTLY ASKED QUESTIONS

FREQUENTLY ASKED QUESTIONS

The following questions are those most frequently asked about HRCI and its certification program. The questions and answers are grouped into the following areas:

- Examination Application
- Examination Preparation
- HR Body of Knowledge
- The Certification Examination
- Examination Administration
- Recertification

EXAMINATION APPLICATION

Q. Why would my application be returned or rejected?

A.   The most common reasons that applications are returned:

- No signature on application forms submitted by mail.
- Not including payment with the application.
- Sending a personal check rather than credit card payment (Visa or Master Card only), money order, cashier's check or organizational check.
- Not including supporting documenation, if needed.
- Submitting a faxed or photo-copied application.
- Not including required forms if applicable, such as the student/recent graduation verification form.

The most common reasons for rejecting an application are:

- Receiving the application after the late registration postmark date.
- Not having two years of exempt-level HR work experience for the examination.

Q. Are examination fees reduced for SHRM members?

A. Yes. HRCI is a separate organization from SHRM. However, SHRM founded HRCI and financed its operations for many years. Today, HRCI is self-supporting. The reduced registration fee for SHRM members is a professional courtesy to SHRM in appreciation for those early years of support.

Q. Why does HRCI require exempt-level HR work experience to be eligible to take the examination?

A. HRCI grants professional certification in the human resource management field. Certification is not granted for paraprofessional or other non-exempt experience. Candidates must have an executive, administrative, or professional exemption under the Fair Labor Standards Act to be eligible for either the PHR or SPHR examination.

Q. Since the eligibility requirements are the same for the PHR and SPHR, how do I determine which exam to take?

A. If you have at least 2-4 years of exempt-level HR work experience, you should consider taking the PHR exam. If you have a broad range of experience/education and 6-8 years of experience, it might be best to take the SPHR. The most important thing is to take the examination that best demonstrates your mastery of the HR body of knowledge.

EXAMINATION PREPARATION

Q. What is the best way to prepare?

A. There is no single best way to prepare. A lot depends on your education and background in the HR field, your learning style and your lifestyle. Select a preparation method that best matches each of these areas. It might be a highly flexible approach, such as individual self-study, or a moderately structured approach, such as a preparation course or the *SHRM® Learning System*. In any case, remember that the examination tests your mastery of the HRCI body of knowledge and it is impossible to teach to the test. Candidates must master the HRCI test specifications and be able to apply it.

Q. Does HRCI recommend learning resources?

A. HRCI does not endorse any one learning resource as being qualitatively better than another. At the same time, those resources based upon the HRCI test specifications may better prepare candidates for the tests.

Q. How do I know if I am ready to take the examination?

A. Review the HRCI test specifications. If you can honestly say that you are comfortable with each of the responsibilities and knowledge areas in the outline, you are probably in pretty good shape to take the examination. It is also a good idea to use a self-assessment and see how you do on the practice questions in this guide.

HR BODY OF KNOWLEDGE

Q. Why are the HRCI test specifications so important?

A. Because it is a blue print for the HRCI examinations. The weightings on the specifications correspond to the weightings on the examination. Candidates will only be tested on subject matter included in the test specifications.

Q. How often does HRCI revise its test specifications?

A. The HR body of knowledge undergoes major revision every five years. Minor revisions occur yearly as a result of expert or literature reviews. Always make sure you are using the current year's HRCI test specifications.

THE CERTIFICATION EXAMINATION

Q. Where do the examination questions come from?

A. Test items are written by certified HR professionals, not by academics or professional test developers. Because the items are developed by certified HR professionals, they tend to be very practical and applied. HRCI examination scores correlate with years of experience and with education.

Q.   How reliable are the examinations?

A.   Very reliable. If you do not pass an examination and decide to retake it without extensive preparation or additional experience, your results will be similar to the first examination.

Q.   Are HRCI examinations validated?

A.   Yes. HRCI examinations are content validated. The blue print for HRCI examinations come from the HRCI test specifications. Those specifications are the result of the HRCI practice analysis process—a sort of job analysis for the entire HR field. Only questions that correspond to the test specifications are used on the examinations. Contributing to this content validation model is the fact that HRCI uses only certified HR professionals to write items, review them, evaluate test forms, and analyze the performance of examinations. HRCI test specifications conform to the highest standards in the certification testing field.

Q.   What is the best predictor of success on the examination?

A.   HR education and exempt-level work experience are the best predictors of success on the HRCI examinations.

Q.   Are examinations administered on one test date easier or more difficult than ones used on another test date?

A.   HRCI uses a statistical procedure called equating to correct any differences in difficulty between different forms of the same test. This equating process results in a scaled score rather than a raw score.

Q.   What is the difference between a raw score and a scaled score?

A.   A raw score is the actual number of items answered correctly on the examination. A scaled score is placed on a uniform scale and reflects differences in difficulty levels of different forms of the same examination. A scaled score ensures that every examinee, no matter when they took the examination, achieves the same uniform standard. A passing score on an HRCI examination is a scaled score of 500. This process ensures consistency and fairness between examination forms.

Q. Are certain functional areas of the examination more difficult than others?

A. The answer is based on the education and experience candidates bring to the examination. For instance, candidates who have never worked in a unionized environment could find items on employee and labor relations more difficult than those with experience in labor relations. It is really an individual matter. Each of the exam's functional areas include questions with a fairly broad range of difficulty levels.

Q. Why are PHR and SPHR examinations weighted differently?

A. PHR and SPHR exams differ in terms of focus and cognitive level of questions. PHR exam questions tend to be at the operational/technical level, and the SPHR questions tend to be at the strategic and/or policy level. Therefore, a major emphasis on the SPHR exam is in strategic management.

Q. Are the questions different between the PHR and SPHR examinations?

A. Yes. PHR questions tend to be technical and operational. They involve the cognitive abilities of recall and comprehension. SPHR questions tend to be more policy-oriented and strategic and test more of the ability to analyze and synthesize, often using scenario questions.

Q. What is a scenario question?

A. A scenario question includes a paragraph (called an information set) that provides basic information about a given situation. It is followed by a series of four answer multiple-choice items. Scenario questions are ideal for the SPHR examination because they require candidates to integrate information from more than one functional area of the HRCI test specifications to arrive at a correct answer. Scenario items reflect situations commonly encountered by senior-level HR practitioners.

Q. Do I have to memorize what year a law was passed?

A. HRCI examinations do not test trivia! It is not important to know what year (1935) the Wagner Act passed, but candidates should know how to identify an unfair labor practice. Remember–HRCI examination questions are very practical and applied.

Q. If I don't know the answer to a question should I leave it blank?

A. No. Scoring is based on the number of correct answers. A guess is far better than leaving a question blank.

EXAMINATION ADMINISTRATION

Q. I have a disability. Can I be accommodated at the examination site?

A. The HRCI certification program complies with the Americans with Disabilities Act covering both facilities and administration. Candidates with special accommodations should submit a request with supporting documentation to the HRCI test vendor at the time of application. Please see the HRCI Certification Information Handbook for more information about these procedures. Handbooks can be requested by calling 1-800-283-7476 or viewed online at **www.hrci.org**.

Q. What if my religion precludes me from Saturday testing?

A. There are special procedures for non-Saturday test administrations including a written request supported by documentation from a clergy member or religious leader. Please see the HRCI Certification Information Handbook for more information about these procedures. Handbooks can be requested by calling 1-800-283-7476 or viewed online at **www.hrci.org**.

Q. Do I need a calculator to take the examination?

A. Examination questions can be answered without the aid of calculators. Calculators are not permitted in the testing center.

Q. What should I do if I fail?

A. Start by reviewing your score report. Score reports with a failing score list the raw scores (number correct) for each of the functional areas. This should help you identify areas that need improvement when considering additional preparation.

Q. Can I have my examination re-scored if I do not pass?

A. Answer sheets that fall within two or three points on either side of the passing score are automatically re-scored by hand. In all the years that HRCI has been administering examinations, it has never encountered a scoring error. If the examination score was not within a couple of points of the passing score and you still want it hand scored, however, that can be arranged for a supplemental fee. Please see the HRCI Certification Information Handbook for more information. Handbooks can be requested by calling 1-800-283-7476 or viewed online at **www.hrci.org**.

Q. Can I review my test booklet or get a list of the questions I missed?

A. Because of test security, test booklets and question/answer documents are not available for review. If you have questions about your examination, direct them to the HRCI examination vendor at the address in the HRCI Certification Information Handbook. All inquiries are reviewed.

RECERTIFICATION

Q. How do I recertify?

A. Recertification is required every three years by the expiration date of the current certification cycle. Recertification can be achieved by successfully retesting or by documenting 60 contact hours of activities that update HR knowledge and/or experience.

Q.   **What education and experience counts toward the 60 contact hours needed for recertification?**

A.   Activities in the following categories can count toward recertification:

Continuing Education
Research and/or Publishing
Instruction
On the-Job Projects
HR Leadership
Professional Membership

An FAQ on recertification and applications are available online at **www.hrci.org**.

Q.   **How was the three-year time frame determined for recertification?**

A.   A recognition by the HRCI Board of the amount and speed of change occurring in the HR field.

Q.   **Why did HRCI do away with lifetime certification for SPHRs?**

A.   The HRCI Board did away with lifetime certification for SPHR's in recognition of the dynamic changes in the HR field. The HRCI Board saw that HR professionals must constantly keep abreast of changing laws and new developments in the field. The HRCI practice analysis process provided the Board an indication of the magnitude of these changes. Technical obsolescence comes quickly in the HR field. Lifetime certification did not reflect the realities of today and was eliminated. Beginning in 1996 and thereafter, newly certified individuals will have to recertify every three (3) years. Those individuals who became SPHR certified through the end of 1995 were grandfathered and are eligible for lifetime certification after recertifying twice.